CULTURE, ANARCHY AND THE PUBLIC SCHOOLS

CULTURE, ANARCHY AND THE PUBLIC SCHOOLS

by

T. E. B. HOWARTH

CASSELL · LONDON

CASSELL & COMPANY LTD
35 RED LION SQUARE, LONDON WC1
Melbourne, Sydney, Toronto
Johannesburg, Auckland

© T. E. B. Howarth 1969
First published 1969

S.B.N. 304 93342 2

Printed in Great Britain by
Cox & Wyman Ltd, London, Fakenham and Reading
F.169

To Frances

CONTENTS

ACKNOWLEDGEMENTS

Thanks are due to the following for permission to reprint copyright material:

Mr C. H. Brown

New English Library Ltd: *The Public Philosophy*—Walter Lippmann

Penguin Books Ltd: *The Comprehensive School*—Robin Pedley

H.M. Stationery Office: *15 to 18, the Report of the Central Advisory Council for Education, England (the Crowther Report)*

Times Newspapers Ltd for letter on page 45 reproduced from *The Times Educational Supplement* and an extract from *The Times Literary Supplement*

Weidenfeld & Nicolson Ltd: *Reform in Education*—James Koerner

PREFACE

A century after the publication of Matthew Arnold's *Culture and Anarchy* my conscious imitation of some of his techniques of exposition and controversy, carried to the point where I have actually purloined one of his chapter headings ('Our Liberal Practitioners'), calls for some explanation. If I succeed in reminding some of my readers of the existence of what Professor Dover Wilson called 'the finest apology for education in the English language' that will perhaps to some extent justify what is sometimes plagiarism though never I hope pastiche. If I have occasionally indulged in what Arnold called 'vivacities', but which might be less favourably described as personalities, my purpose has not been malicious as I hope the tone and purport of my final chapter demonstrate. What I have rather sought to do is to highlight as vividly as possible the fundamental and dangerous divisions that exist today between men and women who are all professionally and personally concerned with the education of the nation's children. Unless we can soon cease tearing ourselves apart in sterile controversy and begin to resolve our differences by the rejection of extremisms it is the children who will suffer most.

Although this book is largely about the public schools it is impossible to isolate questions of their existence and future from the much more pressing problem of the grammar schools and indeed of selection in secondary education. Far the best treatment of this subject is to be found in *The Grammar School* by Robin Davis of Merchant Taylors' School (Penguin Books, 1967). I was also much impressed by Dr James Koerner's

Reform in Education (Weidenfeld, 1968). I am greatly indebted to many colleagues and friends on the Headmasters' Conference. In our deliberations during the past two years we have often had occasion to remember Dr Johnson's proposition that 'when a man knows he is to be hanged in a fortnight, it concentrates his mind wonderfully'. They are not to be held accountable in any way for the views I have expressed in this book. It will be sufficient reward if they are as indulgent with my idiosyncrasies now as they have been in the past.

I should like to express my thanks to Mr John Sparrow for particularly generous help, especially in restraint of my exuberance, and to Mrs Patrick Hutton.

INTRODUCTION

The pursuit of perfection then is the pursuit of sweetness
and light. He who works for sweetness works in the end
for light also; he who works for light works in the end for
sweetness also. But he who works for sweetness and light
united, works to make reason and the will of God prevail.
He who works for machinery, he who works for hatred,
works only for confusion.

Matthew Arnold, *Culture and Anarchy*, 1869

The eloquent climax to a spirited article entitled: 'To Hell
with the Public Schools' in the *New Statesman and Nation* of
21 February 1964 by the publicist John Morgan reads as
follows: 'Public schoolboys seem to find it difficult to com-
prehend—I want to be cool and reasonable about this—the
hysterical rage, the inarticulate fury, that the existence of
independent, fee-paying schools can inspire. I have friends
who have to be given something to bite on when confronted,
as one is almost daily, with news that some clown has been
appointed to a job in business, journalism or politics, by virtue
of his belonging to the public school class. This almost hydro-
phobic response is not envy. Who, after all, could envy anyone,
of either sex, the miseries and deprivations of a public school
education? ... A dramatic act of abolition, with a ceremonial
detonation or two, would be deeply satisfying. No other single
gesture could knock off so many targets.' When the young—
or not so young—lions of the *New Statesman* roar with this
degree of vehemence they set up fearful vibrations and echoes.
Confronted with the more strident of the political reformers
of a century ago Matthew Arnold liked to remind his readers
of the maxims of the eighteenth-century Bishop of Sodor and

Man, Thomas Wilson. Even in our day we can usefully recall one of the Bishop's observations which might have been expressly framed for Mr Morgan—'intemperance in talk makes a dreadful havoc in the heart'. But Mr Morgan is by no means a lone voice. A recent writer in the *Morning Star* was certainly not bearing Bishop Wilson's maxim in mind when he forecast that if the Public Schools Commission had its way 'the playing fields of Eton will continue to train our upper class élite to muck up the economy and keep the workers in their place'.[1] No sweetness there assuredly; and perhaps a little more light might have suggested that statesmen other than those educated at Eton could be criticized from time to time in language of comparable elegance for what they do to the economy. The cut and thrust of parliamentary debate is a fine thing and a stout preservative of British liberty. When, however, the Rt Hon. Patrick Gordon Walker, lately Secretary of State for Education and Science, with a sharp flash of wit observed that 'the preservation and restoration of selection in education has taken the place of hanging and flogging as the war-cry of the Ancient Britons in the Tory Party', he might be thought to have done better to remember Bishop Wilson's golden rule: 'Firstly, never go against the best light you have; secondly, take care that your light be not darkness.' For Mr Gordon Walker knows very well, as a former Oxford don, that at some stage in education there must be selection. He may legitimately hope that in a large, purpose-built, well organized comprehensive school with an outstanding headmaster, it may be postponed for a time without harming anybody very much; he should know by now that in hastily improvised schemes of comprehensive schooling it is exceedingly important to select children and arrange them into appropriate groups as soon as possible if lasting damage is not to be done to the very slow and also to the very quick children.

One of the surest ways of not diffusing either sweetness or light is to have a tendency to underrate the complexity of

---

[1] 19 February 1968.

complex issues, to be what the French call *un terrible simplifica-teur*. The National Union of Teachers is a body of educated men and women. Just how many of its 287,000 members would wish to endorse the evidence presented in their name to the Public Schools Commission is an interesting speculation. The evidence in question concludes as follows: 'The Union can only recommend total integration. Some will claim that this means "the abolition of the public schools". The Union does not flinch from this interpretation. It believes that the social problem posed by the public school is so serious to the com-munity at large, that it cannot be ignored, that a partial or temporizing solution cannot be permanent and that accord-ingly it is better to support a radical solution even if it is hard. Of course there will be opposition and the opposition will be encouraged by vested interests of many kinds; but we believe a radical solution, if firmly explained and firmly held in face of criticism will win wide support.' It is admirable and in the best British tradition not to flinch when confronted with a serious problem and the Union goes out of its way to tell us that it is not flinching. However, the attitude of the general public to root-and-branch solutions to social problems can sometimes be very disappointing to even the most confident of reformers. How much support *does* the proposal to abolish the public schools command in the country? Opinions on matters of this sort are no doubt very volatile these days and opinion polls are periodically fallible. Even so, within a very few months, the Union Executive's confident conviction that their well-publicized proposals would win *wide* support may have been somewhat undermined by an opinion poll organized by the *Sunday Times*. Six per cent of the replies supported abolition of the public schools; 21% supported some plan 'to bring them into the state system'; 7% had no view on the subject; 67% preferred to leave the schools as they are. It will be recalled, furthermore, that the majority report of the Public Schools Commission[1] was not received with marked public

---

[1] *See* Appendix, p. 93.

3

acclamation. Admittedly, it was insufficiently radical for the National Union of Teachers, but it did not, on the other hand, call forth any great enthusiasm of response from more moderate reformers. Now there are times when the formers of public opinion are well ahead of the community and the community does well to lend an ear to their prophetic tones. But again there are times when the formers of public opinion are just not getting through to the community at all and do their best to console themselves in the words of the Book of Lamentations: 'Thou hast heard my voice; hide not thine ear at my breathing.'

It is always advisable when great reform movements are in the air to analyse the employment of the word *radical*, as used for instance in the term 'radical solution'. John Roebuck was a great nineteenth-century Radical with a notable record for assiduity in promoting commissions of inquiry, but for all his good works he was notoriously tiring. Matthew Arnold observed of him that he was perpetually asking the happily rhetorical question: 'May not every man in England say what he likes?' and went on to write: 'When every man may say what he likes, our aspirations ought to be satisfied. But the aspirations of culture, which is the study of perfection, are not satisfied, unless what men say, when they may say what they like, is worth saying.' It will be noted that the solution to the public school problem from which the National Union of Teachers (or their Executive) does not flinch is a radical one. But then curiously the quite different and much more moderate solution offered by the majority of the Public Schools Commission is introduced with the words 'we believe that the wise course of action at this moment of time is to press ahead with a scheme which is indeed radical'. Again an organization called the Socialist Educational Association prefaces its pamphlet on the public schools with a quotation from a work of the Rt Hon. Anthony Crosland's in 1962—'We must have either a radical reform or none at all.' Evidently the one thing needful these days is to have radical solutions.

The trouble, however, with radical solutions to social prob-

4

lems in complex industrial societies is that it is seldom easy to isolate one particular sector of the whole field. If you desire to single out for especially radical treatment the education of other people's children according to *a priori* doctrinal considerations about which there is no general consensus of opinion you may easily provoke very intense opposition. You will be wise at any rate before putting your hand to an exercise in radical social engineering in this field to ensure that you have adequately surveyed your foundations, worked out your costings and above all made sure that your superstructures are not so heavy that the resultant stresses are such as to bring the building down round your ears. Since education is essentially concerned with human beings there will always be an element of unpredictability about the consequences of educational reform. It is of course no argument against the creation of a large number of small new universities that their emergence should have coincided with the most massive demonstration of student unrest since the eighteen-forties, but had such a development been even remotely suspected the new universities might have been very differently planned. When the present administration set out to reorganize secondary education along radical and expensive lines it may not have anticipated that the Plowden Commission's report would soon emerge, demonstrating irrefutably that conditions in the primary sector imperatively demanded in terms of basic human justice the first call on whatever resources were available. Again it can hardly have been anticipated by Mr Wedgwood Benn as he went out of his way to commend the necessity for all secondary education to become fully comprehensive as rapidly as possible that he might one day read in *New Society* (10 October 1968) an article headed 'Our Class-Ridden Comprehensives', the outcome of a research study by Miss Julienne Ford which appears to demonstrate that class distinctions are more rigid in comprehensive schools than they were in the much discredited tripartite system. No doubt such a totally unexpected demonstration of the difficulty of expelling nature with a pitchfork will be much modified in due course but it at least suggests that the human factor in matters of educational reform is such that it is a mistake to be too hot for certainties. In recent years most people in educational circles, whatever their differences, have derived much satisfaction from the fact that the old sectarian quarrels which disfigured the educational scene for over a hundred years have abated. The attitude of the High Church clergyman who proclaimed that 'he would never permit an emissary of Lord John Russell, or any other Turkish Bashaw, to enter his school' or the furious agitation against what was called 'Rome on the rates' are things of the past. Is it then wise today to preach schemes of radical reform in education with sometimes excessive ideological fervour in a situation where there is nothing like a consensus of opinion on matters which can easily arouse a bitter clash of wills since they affect people's children? Since education in this country is essentially a partnership between the central and the local authorities it would not seem particularly desirable to accentuate the political aspects of educational controversy unless you can be reasonably sure that there will be sufficient political congruity between Whitehall and the local authorities. Education cannot possibly be taken out of politics but it will surely be the statesmanlike action to be always seeking for solutions which are reasonably bi-partisan and which make for peaceful coexistence. Thus if we believe, as many, though by no means all the inhabitants of these islands do, that equality is what we are after it will be sensible to formulate that ideal as uncontroversially as possible, as for instance with the proposition that equality means equal opportunity to develop unequally. When, however, in practical terms you have to ask the further question at what age and under what arrangements the process of developing unequally should begin there is room for much argument and much genuine difference of opinion. Even to ask the question is to be confronted with the one unassailable proposition in all educational theory, namely that all children and all the families of which they form part are different. It was this intractable problem which in a sense defeated the well-meaning framers of the 1944 Education Act, who devised a scheme for children whereby they should all be either grammar children or modern children or technical children. We may be sensible to conclude before erecting new systems and new machinery that we should whenever possible inform the debate with common sense and the will to agree amongst ourselves. Hydrophobia and hanging and flogging will be better kept out of the discussion.

CHAPTER 1
EQUALITY AND ÉLITISM

Human nature demands, no doubt, space and elbow-room. But there is an excellence of repose and contentment, as well as of effort; and, happily, the mass of mankind are not all elbows. If they possess powers which call for the opportunity to assert themselves in the contests of the market-place, and to reap the reward of successful rivalry, they have also qualities, which, though no less admirable, do not find their perfection in a competitive struggle, and the development of which is no less indispensable to social health. Equality of opportunity implies the establishment of conditions which favour the expansion, not, as societies with a strong economic bent are disposed to believe, of the former alone, but of both. Rightly interpreted, it means not only that what are commonly regarded as the prizes of life should be open to all, but that none should be subjected to arbitrary penalties; not only that exceptional men should be free to exercise their exceptional powers, but that common men should be free to make the most of their common humanity. If a community which is indifferent to the need of facilitating the upward movement of ability becomes torpid and inert, a community which is indifferent to all else but that movement becomes hardened and materialized. . . .

R. H. Tawney

Upon the whole, I think that what little can be truly said of equality is that as a fact human beings are not equal; that in their dealings with each other they ought to recognize real inequalities where they exist as much as substantial equality when it exists.

James Fitzjames Stephen

One 30 April a few years ago I was caught in the streets of

Paris by a particularly violent thunderstorm. As I dived into a taxi by one door a thin, hawk-nosed and evidently blue-blooded Frenchman entered it by the other door. We agreed to share the taxi in our common misfortune. Though the English are brought up never to talk to strangers, the French are not, so I ventured a few remarks about the likelihood of the weather ruining the May Day celebrations the following morning. My companion replied caustically: 'C'est le bon Dieu qui crache sur le prolétariat.' It is difficult to imagine that this somewhat anti-Dreyfusard observation would ever occur to an Englishman, however well 'connected', yet we are often told that Britain suffers uniquely from a rigid, archaic stratification of society by class. In much up-to-date writing we can expect to find the phrase 'our class-ridden society'. Writers on this theme as they warm to it often display considerable ingenuity. Thus the critic Mr D. A. N. Jones describes an actress playing Queen Victoria with the phrase 'she has the amused, slurring drawl of a modern landowner'. Not everyone has the opportunity these days to study the speech-patterns of modern landowners but we all think we know what we mean when we use the word 'élite' or 'élitist'. It will be characteristic of the élitist that he will hold down the progress of the technological society; that he will 'jealously preserve privilege'; that he will have an unaccountable enthusiasm for shooting game birds and eating them in a relatively advanced state of decomposition. In educational circles if somebody wishes particularly to brand you as archaic and out of touch with the march of progress they will call you not only an élitist but a Platonist. Leaving Plato aside, as we must if we are to keep abreast of the Socialist Educational Association with their observation that 'Latin and Greek are useless knowledge, and useless knowledge is the hall-mark of a gentleman', we may still do well to take a slightly closer look at the concept of élitism. Georges Clemenceau, who in a long life-time destroyed a remarkable number of conservative French cabinets and was once known as the Red Mayor of Montmartre, concluded that there was a rather special, if often unheeded, connection between élitism and the proper functioning of democracy.

> Democracy [he said] is not demagogy. Demagogy does not mean the permanent and unchangeable equality of all individuals. If it did, one would have before one only two solutions to the problem of the state and of government; either anarchy pure and simple, or the election of all government officials by drawing lots. That latter system was practised in Athens, but you know as well as I do that that was for show; the real rulers were not the authorities who had been chosen by lot. No, democracy is essentially the régime in which people are governed by élites. Find the best way of forming élites—that is the essential problem of democracy. The régime should be such that the élite could be drawn from all sections of the nation. Extend the intelligent sections of the upper classes; infiltrate them by extending the intelligent sections of the lower, so that the rulers will come back to their point of departure and will lead in a direction that may be acceptable to and practicable by the nation as a whole. Whatever a country's form of government may be, it will always end by falling into bureaucracy unless it is dominated by exceptional personalities.

If there is anything in this point of view, we may consider that élitism is not after all such a totally ignoble approach to the problem which presses on all of us—namely how to improve the quality of life in a Western democracy. There are of course many other approaches. The Provost of King's in the Reith Lectures which may transpire to be the funeral oration of the permissive society (or alternatively its charter of liberties) appeared to hold that what we have to do is to eliminate the influence of the middle-aged and loosen the bonds of the family. The satire industry sustains the view that as long as we retain a paranoid attitude to the Establishment all should be well in time. Popular singers and their managers seek to remind us—and how right in a way they are—that much can be achieved by what they call love. Radical students in the streets propound more violent solutions. There is very general support for the idea that we should be always intent on moving towards the classless society, though the awkward question of just what are the norms of the classless society to which we ought to be moving—a legitimate question in a sense, since there is no historical record of any such society—is never very satisfactorily answered, nor for that matter sufficiently frequently asked.

If then one is to do anything so unfashionable as to seek a reconsideration of the concept of élitism amid this general ferment of new ideas, one has to tread warily and indeed be prepared to risk the exposure of some unpalatable truths. 'Extend the intelligent sections,' says Clemenceau. Before one can discuss such an idea fruitfully it will be important to clear the ground carefully in relation to certain advanced, popular and attractive ideas now much in vogue. No less an authority than Sir John Newsom himself has observed: 'there are no unintelligent children, only unintelligent teachers'. Reinforcing this proposition, we hear from Siegfried and Theresa Engelmann in their book *Give Your Child a Superior Mind* (Frewin, 1968) that 'all healthy children are intelligent'. It may be that when Sir John Newsom and Siegfried and Theresa Engelmann use the word 'intelligent' they mean 'capable of conceptual thought', which even if it be only at a low level is the great glory of *homo sapiens*. It is important, however, to distinguish this very clearly from the idea that every child is able to manage the differential calculus or to disentangle and hold in his mind the complexities of the Eastern Problem in the nineteenth century or to appreciate the sublimities of *King Lear*.

The environmentalists are all the rage these days, emphasizing the all-importance of nurture and having nothing to do with innate natural qualities or the influence of parental genes. Indeed, it would be a stupid and crassly insensitive person who did not accept the fact that deprivation in early childhood is a major deterrent to effective education. To combat it we need better nursery, infant and primary schools and antecedent to that better homes. Yet when all is said and done—and a great deal needs to be done—common sense overwhelmingly suggests that some boys and girls have a superior native endowment to others. Indeed, it is sometimes immensely superior. We have moved on in the sophistication of our society since the days when Lord Melbourne sought to impede a measure for increased public education by saying: 'Look at the Paget family. None of them can read or write, yet they manage well enough.' We demand—and rightly—that everyone should read and write and indeed read and write as well as he or she can or is inclined to. We may also feel, as Clemenceau did, that our culture and our economy will be likely to benefit if we make sure that we train our brighter boys and girls to the pitch of perfection of which they are capable, so that the full range of their talents can be deployed for the benefit of the community and so that in due course, as R. H. Tawney puts it, exceptional men should be free to exercise their exceptional powers. To take an example, it is rare but not unknown for a quite small child to evince an early genius at playing the piano. Only a few fanatics for equality would think it particularly sensible to immure such a child in a classful of contemporaries engaged in five-finger exercises or that happy, if not invariably harmonious, activity known in primary schools as 'percussion'. Yet any attempt to differentiate between children's abilities in matters of number or language will arouse passionate cries of 'élitist' or 'Platonist'.

The agony arises in part from a certain confusion arising from the word élite itself. Whatever Clemenceau had in mind when he warned us that without élites democracy collapses into bureaucracy, he certainly was not thinking of an élite based exclusively on wealth and birth. The argument does not centre primarily round the desirability or otherwise of perpetuating a race of languid duchesses or intrepid deer-stalkers. We can happily rely on Mr Will Hamilton, M.P., with his anxious concern for the economy of Buckingham Palace, to guard us from perils of that sort. 'Extend the intelligent section of the upper classes; infiltrate them by extending the intelligent sections of the lower,' says Clemenceau. On the face of it an unexceptionable programme, though it will immediately be suggested that intelligence is not all. What about character? Is it not generally felt that the English have a proper distrust of the intellect? Indeed, the public schools have been widely criticized for displaying an exaggerated concern for the process known as character-building. They are frequently told that their ethos is exclusively directed towards the inculcation of leadership qualities as a preparation for imperial administration (never, as it happened, qualities of a totally unintellectual nature) at a time when there is no longer an empire. Nevertheless, both character and leadership qualities continue to matter.

If it were considered, as it well might be, that a Fellowship of the Royal Society is the hallmark of a leader in contemporary society it is of some relevance that the school with most Fellows of the Royal Society to its credit is Winchester with sixteen, followed by St Paul's with ten and Manchester Grammar School with nine. But if we were to try and read too much into this we would need to pay some attention to the enthusiasts of the Socialist Educational Association, who tell us, under the presidency of the Rt Hon. Anthony Greenwood, that 'the breach between pure science and applied science stems directly from the public school insistence on pure learning for its own sake; on the traditional classical curriculum'. This is of course brisk and progressive comment and certainly there is a great and mounting demand for applied scientists of all sorts and especially engineers, though presumably not even the Socialist Educational Association would in any way wish to stem the flow of good pure scientists. Supporters of the public schools, however, can derive some comfort from the fact that in 1967 easily the most popular intended career of public school leavers was engineering with 11·3% (followed by pure science with 7·4%). If the sort of leadership qualities inculcated in the pupils had some relevance in the past to imperial administration we may hope that, always aware of the strictures of the Socialist Association, the schools may find it equally possible to provide their appropriate quota to the technical élite of the engineering industry.

We may then go on to ask whether it is not true that the most dangerous intellectual is the frustrated one whom circumstances at home or in the school or the university have continued to retard and to warp and to embitter. If we are concerned with the character qualities of our young intellectuals, boys and girls, it will be sensible to give them their heads early. But let us be wary in any case of supporting too readily the traditional English dichotomy between character and intellect. There is a mood about these days which seeks to decry educational qualifications, examinations and anything which suggests that some are perhaps cleverer than others. It will be argued that if they are cleverer, this is because they have been quite improperly luckier than others and that in particular examinations are no test of character and are always to be dismissed as something called a rat-race. Clearly, indeed, if you need to demonstrate that everybody is equal or ought to be continually striving to that end then you do well not to have examinations. Yet it is perhaps worth reflecting for a moment on an observation of Mr Gladstone's when he was supporting the principle of educational qualifications for entry to the Civil Service in a letter to Queen Victoria: 'experience at the Universities and Public Schools of this country has shown that in a large majority of cases the test of open examination is also an effectual test of character. . . . The previous industry and self-denial . . . are rarely separated from general habits of virtue.'

Neither the English grammar school nor the English public school was or is a perfect institution, but the best of them would not seem on any sensible view of the matter institutions we should seek to destroy in that they have no inconsiderable record in bringing on the talents of able children and are capable of even further development in that wholly desirable social purpose. A consideration of how the nation might best utilize these resources by applying (and not a minute too soon) the sovereign criterion of common sense can best be left to the concluding chapter. At this stage in the argument, however, it seems sensible to advance a few preliminary observations.

However much criticism can be levelled at the first Report of the Public Schools Commission it establishes in its survey of the public boarding schools beyond any argument that, to quote its own words, 'they are an important part of the nation's secondary education system'. We shall need, therefore, to examine carefully whether the 'radical' proposals it suggests are a sensible exploitation of that educational capital in the national interest—that is if we feel, as we may, that in matters of this sort common sense as well as radicalism is to have its say. The Public Schools Commission, reorganized and refurbished, is now to examine with equal vigour and no doubt equal radicalism the independent day schools and among others great direct grant grammar schools like Manchester Grammar School, King Edward's School, Birmingham, Bristol Grammar School, Bradford Grammar School, Brentwood School, Leeds Grammar School and the academically outstanding Girls Public Day School Trust institutions. It will be surprising if at the end of their deliberations the Commissioners do not find that these schools also constitute 'an important part of the nation's secondary education system'. It is a sobering, though not altogether fanciful, speculation that the Commissioners may conclude that the trouble with these particular schools is that they are *too* good and are therefore in urgent need of adjustment to enable them to conform more nearly to the average.

Why, one may well ask, are such schools under attack and why is it considered an almost unspeakable human defect to have élitist tendencies? This state of affairs is largely the work of a force in society which we may call Edmass and which repays some critical scrutiny.

CHAPTER 2
EDMASS

The teaching profession differs, perhaps fortunately, perhaps unfortunately, from other professions such as law or medicine or dentistry in the huge volume of advice available to its practitioners from experts not themselves directly involved in the actual process of teaching. Naturally an activity absorbing so much of the national income will require a great many officials operating complex administrative machinery. Again there will be a need for many persons to involve themselves in the training of teachers, the inspection of schools, the ordering of examinations, the publication of textbooks and many other necessary auxiliary services. A huge and expanding industry has grown up on the periphery of the teaching profession. Why people other than professional administrators choose this form of life may at first seem surprising. Some have for a time been teachers. They may have felt the financial rewards too meagre or their ambitions not quite coming to fruition, or they may have found that through some more or less distressing personal defect they were not successful at managing children. Generally, however, they are characterized by a great zeal for the propagation of their ideas, their researches, perhaps even occasionally their prejudices. I say generally because there is always the exception like the director of a Department of Education in one of our ancient universities whose notorious disillusionment with some of the matters with which he was concerned even permeated his obituary notice in *The Times*: 'He was a scholar,' wrote his obituarist, 'troubled by the duty of education and overwhelmed by the task of administration, much of which he knew was a heaping of paper on paper to the confusion of the world.' As a rule we may, however, hope such an attitude not to be representative of the host of high-minded and well-meaning experts behind the teaching front line whom we may liken in their indispensability to what is called the tail of a modern army, ranging from the strategic planners to the Mobile Bath Units.

This large corps of professional advisers, which we may for brevity's sake call Edmass, tends to follow transatlantic fashion, though in this, as in other respects, we are sometimes less self-critical than are the Americans themselves in our palpable anxiety not to be thought in any way outmoded. Thus in his book *The House of Intellect* (Secker and Warburg, 1962), Professor Jacques Barzun (not himself an American by origin but Dean of Faculties and Provost of Columbia University) writes of educational research: 'There is as a matter of fact no such science. The results are vitiated in advance by the non-existence of the entities they refer to. No doubt the children observed, the events counted, the test papers scored, are genuine objects in the world of experience; but the generalities inferred from them are either tendentious or tautological. . . . Human capacity is more varied than educational researchers know, though their methods ensure that they shall never find this out.' As a characteristic example of how Edmass can occasionally blind us with the profundity of its research findings, he quotes Paul V. Gump and Jacob S. Kounin of Wayne State University who discovered that 'a high firmness correction, such as a proper reprimand accompanied by leading the child by the hand or looking at him pointedly had a salutary effect on other misbehaviour-bent children in the group'. Mr Gump and Mr Kounin went on to observe that 'high-clarity' statements such as 'don't take away the blocks when Johnny's using them' were more effective than 'low-clarity' statements such as 'stop it!' This particular mode of thought and expression, which we may loosely call Gumpishness, is a by no means uncommon phenomenon in Edmass publications. Generally we may find that the constituent elements of Gumpishness in the world of Edmass are the following:

18

1. An unnecessary obscurity of language.
2. An almost compulsive concern with the obvious.
3. Heavy work with the data.
4. A subjective and 'progressive' conclusion.

An Edmass textbook which particularly repays study in these respects is a book recently published called *Looking Forward to the Seventies* (C. Smythe, 1968), sub-titled (characteristically) 'A Blueprint for Education'. It has twenty-five contributors, not all Edmass men, whom the editor describes as 'individuals whose eminence in the field of education is unchallenged'. Here are some illustrations of our four principles of Gumpishness:

1. 'It is really a huge umbrella under which anything progressive can be implemented.' (Lord Butler on the 1944 Education Act.)
2. 'As Talleyrand remarked: "Those who did not live before the revolution will never know how sweet life is."' (Sir Ronald Gould, lately secretary of the N.U.T., being much more progressive than even Talleyrand, whose celebrated remark about the *douceur de vivre* was applied to life as it was *before* the revolution—in other words for 'is' read 'was'.)
3. 'There is one piece of evidence which I must mention though it appears to outweigh much of the anti-streaming opinion and research. The N.F.E.R.[1] report contained the results of an opinion survey among parents and teachers. It alleged that most parents and teachers were *in favour* of streaming. But it is my contention that if parents and teachers were fully aware of all the evidence, they would *not* favour it.' (Bruce Kemble, Education Reporter of the *Daily Express*.)
4. 'A policy of community development posits, first, active recipients of whatever is publicly provided; second, co-operation between statutory authorities, between

---

[1] National Foundation for Educational Research.

voluntary organizations and individuals, and between both; third, economic use of resources; fourth, greater flexibility in occupational attitudes, leading to inter-professional mobility; and lastly, the involvement of as large a part of the community as possible in its own improvement. The problem for educational policy is to decide in what way, by what instruments and agencies, by what combination of provided and secured resources and at what points its efforts are to be directed. Above all, schemes must match the capacities of practitioners and the realities of situations. It is necessary to know what forms have already emerged of inter-departmental co-operation and of integration of effort between different individuals, institutions and phases of education, before a sound estimate can be made of the prospects for a flexible inter-professional relationship in future.' (E. Parkinson apparently exemplifying Parkinson's Law in Edmass.)

5. 'The terms in current use are not the happiest. There is a good deal of confusion between "Liberal" and "General" and terms like "Liberal Studies" can be provocative as well as meaningless. In some quarters "General" seems to have been a retreat from the consequences of "Liberal". It was a retreat from the frying-pan. "Liberal" may be difficult but "General" is too general.' (Ibid.)

6. 'Exhorters and advisers need opportunities and persuasion to re-learn on the ground the practical context of their recommendations.' (Ibid.)

What one might call the heavier Edmass is by now an international industry which has gained great momentum over the years. If one dips, for instance, into the *Year Book of Education* of 1961, a publication with many international contributors concerned with the education of gifted children, one is told with appropriate scientific rigour that 'perceptions, parental attitudes and community attitudes are associated variables that require scrutiny'; or again that 'as a learning concept, enrichment is neither horizontal nor vertical, but circular and spiral'; or 'no school, not even the Gymnasium, can nowadays reveal to a young person the world as it actually exists'. It can perhaps be imagined that literature of this sort, however well subsidized, has a limited readership.

Hitherto we have been concerned with what might be called heavy Edmass. Heavy Edmass is of course immensely influential and ever earnestly striving after professional and academic status. We now have degrees known as B.Eds. and M.Eds. It may well be that we even have D.Eds.—if not we soon will.[1] But just as in the van of an army there is heavy cavalry and light cavalry, so in the van of progressive education there is heavy Edmass and light Edmass.

Light Edmass has about it a less portentous and much lighter tone. Whereas heavy Edmass derives largely from institutions like UNESCO, Departments of Education and Institutes of Education, light Edmass is more journalistic and polemical. Where heavy Edmass more often seeks to instruct teachers and to maintain a spirited technical dialogue between its own *cognoscenti*, light Edmass ventures boldly forth to tell parents what they should be doing with their children and to enlighten the general public about everything that is most enlightened, though at times it is not always guiltless of indulging itself in what the French call *bourrage de crâne*. An advanced spearhead of light Edmass is the organization known as the Advisory Centre for Education in Cambridge, a flourishing enterprise with a most influential director in Mr Brian Jackson. Here from the columns of the *Sunday Times* magazine section is Mr Jackson in the best avuncular light Edmass vein answering the following tricky question—'My

---

[1] Just as there is strong pressure for all teachers to be, like general practitioners, part of one professional body. No doubt very laudable, though if as a result we all had to be part of one N.U.T. closed shop the project would be deficient in its appeal to the liberal-minded.

c

15-year-old son, now at progressive school, where to work or not is left to him, chooses not to work. He says he misses the marking system of his prep school, where he always came near the top of his form. Do some children need to be spurred on in this way?' Answer, by Mr Brian Jackson—'I can't make out what you're up to. Do you mean to say that you sent your boy to a mark-hungry prep school where the pupils were ranked and graded all the time? And now you've turned your ideas upside down and sent him to a school where it's up to him whether he works or not? And little more than a year later you're puzzled because he's puzzled at his new personal responsibility? Sounds perfectly natural to me. If I'd been ground in some examination mill till I was 13, and then released into one of the major progressive schools like Bedales or Dartington Hall, I should think it would be so exciting—leisure, girls, book browsing, woods, music and just sheer play —that it would be hard to value "work" at all. Obviously your boy isn't really missing "work" (what *does* that word mean?) since you say the school offers him the choice and he turns it down. All he is missing is the mark system, the medal-pinning, the illusory clarity of learning and growth.' Encouraging for Dartington Hall; but there will be some who will still in their unenlightened way cling to the illusory clarity of learning and growth and will be perfectly clear in their minds about the meaning of the word 'work'.

Light Edmass, as one might expect, not infrequently involves television and radio. Thus the B.B.C.'s Fyfe Robertson will be found rhapsodizing about free activity schools which he will contrast with 'hide-bound grammar school feed-them-facts authoritarians', a remarkable example of the sort of colourful generalization which does little to help serious public discussion of these far from simple issues. Another vigorous practitioner of light Edmass is Mr Christopher Price, M.P., who edits an organ called *New Education* which has been through some vicissitudes since its inception. Among his many anxieties one of the most pressing is his persistent fear that headmasters tend to be dictatorial like George III or Robespierre or Lenin.

With his liberal proclivities he would like to see schools run on a more generally consultative basis. 'One feature which I am particularly unhappy about,' he says, 'is the pure Matthew Arnold image, in which most headmasters of schools see themselves.' Matthew Arnold was of course an inspector of schools and not a headmaster, yet one sees well enough what Mr Price is concerned about. Even more trenchant is Mr Kai Ehlers, who contributes to the Bulletin of the General Studies Association[1] and is described as having 'studied and visited schools in the U.S.S.R.' and as having 'lived in Germany and Central Europe'. His view is that 'The English headmaster is one of the lasting monuments to English amateurism—perhaps even more lamentable is the way in which they are arbiters of the school curriculum when the vast majority of them do not even understand the language of the argument'. All the same, schools are, or should be, busy places and if policy decisions have frequently to be referred to a common room committee there is always the possibility, schoolmasters being what they are, of divided counsels, if not of total deadlock or intolerable delays in the decision making process. Indeed, the greatest living hero of light Edmass, Mr Albert Rowe of the David Lister Comprehensive School, who has by now had more publicity than any headmaster anywhere since Thomas Arnold, during one of his frequent Press interviews[2] commented very roughly about that formidable co-operative enterprise, the Schools Council: 'Lot of committees. Don't you know the joke, a camel is a horse designed by a committee?' However, he has the advantage of having a staff mostly under thirty, finding young teachers 'more malleable, more imaginative, more likely to reject the élitist system'. Anybody who knows Mr Rowe even slightly would readily accept that he is exactly what Clemenceau would have called 'an exceptional personality', but if he is not careful light Edmass will make a laughing stock of him if they go on suggesting all the

---

[1] Spring 1968.
[2] *The Times Educational Supplement*, 8 March 1968.

time that everything he touches invariably turns to educational gold.

Light Edmass has its other folk heroes. There is Mr Michael Young, whose strictures on what he calls the 'meritocracy' have succeeded in developing a curiously persistent myth in this country that merit is something to be both eschewed and unrewarded. There is Professor Robin Pedley, a veteran crusader for the cause of comprehensive schools, whose singleminded zeal has nearly succeeded in destroying the English grammar school.

> The large American high school is no longer primarily a part of the local community, but a self-sufficient community on its own. The staff are fully absorbed in their important, ever-changing, and always demanding work. Not only are there departments staffed by specialists for all the normal subjects; there is also a guidance department run by qualified psychologists whose job it is to assess the personality and ability of each pupil and to help him to choose both the right path through school, with its multitude of options, and the right career on leaving school. . . . The great educational debate in North America . . . is about the grouping of children *within* the common school. At present there is little more than the occasional attempt to put the clever children in one class or stream, the average in a second, the slow in a third, and so on. . . . Within a broad curriculum, there is room for much individual choice. Rapid progress in a favourite subject can take a pupil into a class one or two grades higher for that subject, while he pursues others at a more normal pace . . . (America) believes that the great contributions to human life have come from individuals who were allowed or were determined to assert their unique view-point, often flatly against the weight of orthodox opinion. Copernicus, Martin Luther, Charles Darwin, and beyond them Jesus of Nazareth —theirs is the spirit that inspires the thought and works of America's educators from Dewey to Conant.

On this Dr James D. Koerner, an American expert, tartly comments in his recent work *Reform in Education*: 'Not even the American Association of School Administration would suppose that such an uninformed assessment, sans any mention of standards or achievement, of the American school has any resemblance to reality'. Then there is Mr Max Morris, another comprehensive headmaster (Willesden High School) with exceptionally progressive views who hailed the year 1967 as one 'full of promise and excitement' for education. 'It was the year in which the teaching profession began to get off its knees and the comprehensive programme began to get off the ground. It was the year when the main body of the teaching profession at long last demanded the end of the public schools, the most retarding influence on genuine public education in Britain.'[1] An alternative view might be that the most retarding influence on genuine public education is the fact that if Mr Morris has his way all the children whose parents cannot afford to pay for an alternative in the 'catchment area' of Willesden High School will have to go to his school, a pattern to be uniformly imposed throughout the country. 'Comprehensive education is irresistible,' says Mr Morris. It is always the mark of the *terrible simplificateur* to argue that since history is on his side he must be right.

Inevitably involved in the activities of Edmass, more often in its lighter rather than its heavier aspects, are the educational journalists. Being a journalist in modern society or indeed for some centuries has been a desperately heavy responsibility and one that has not always earned public gratitude. Kierkegaard tells us in his diary that he always wanted to shoot any journalist at sight. Most educational journalists in this country are as a matter of fact in the highest degree fair and responsible. Their troubles stem of course from the terrible necessity under which they labour to make education news. It is not news when thousands of boys and girls are working away in their chemistry laboratories, nor by now even when they are working away in their language laboratories. The difficulty is to find something different going on in schools. The more popular

---

[1] *The Times Educational Supplement*, 26 January 1968

journalists of course occasionally get a windfall which they will be able to set out like this: 'Boys scuttled from their dormitories in the small hours of Tuesday as a deafening explosion shook the rafters of Middlefriars, one of England's exclusive public schools (fees £625; motto "Impavidum Ferient Ruinae").' Fortunately, *pace* Mr John Morgan, such incidents are comparatively rare. Inevitably, however, there will be a tendency among all educational reporters to seek out that which is novel and experimental and, among some, that which is politically sensational. This in turn provides a perfect platform from which the light Edmass men in the van of progress can succeed in familiarizing the general public with even the most bizarre theories, so that in quite a short time they become accepted as self-evident truths. The effect of all this on parents anxious to do the best they can for their children under bewildering new conditions can well be envisaged. They are continually taught to conclude that if their child is streamed at school his future will be in jeopardy; that if they pay for his education they are being anti-social; that they ought continually to involve themselves in parental committees so that they can oversee the headmaster; and that if they send their child to a single-sex school he or she will be ruined for life. Indeed, if they really study their A. S. Neill (the *Sunday Times*, 26 November 1967) they may begin to wonder whether in their children's interests they shouldn't become nudists—'the children from a nudist home must meet many children who have the wrong ideas and feelings about sex. Since children hate to be outside a group, the ones from sensible homes may find it hard to stand aloof'.

As a personal contribution to the literature of light Edmass I consoled myself during some of the less rewarding moments of the Public Schools Commission by drawing up the following imaginary report of a visit to St Paul's by the Commissioners, which may serve to focus the reader's attention on some of the more characteristic Edmass attitudes to traditional education.

PUBLIC SCHOOLS COMMISSION

A VISIT TO ST PAUL'S SCHOOL

Governors
A disturbing feature of the government of this highly selective and in many ways anachronistic institution is the number of governors whose primary concern is with higher education. Pending a long-term solution, two possibilities suggest themselves. The present Dean of St Paul's being of a particularly ripe age might be persuaded to resign, which would have the added advantage of severing the link with the Cathedral which, being over four hundred years old, would seem to be serving no particular purpose under the changed conditions of today. At the same time it is scarcely in accordance with contemporary trends for the school to be governed by a member of so overtly meritocratic an institution as the London School of Economics. Strong neighbourhood links could be forged if the governors concerned were replaced by representatives of the White City and the Hammersmith Palais de Danse. A further vacancy might in due course be allotted to a representative of Wormwood Scrubs or some other liberal and outgoing institution in the neighbourhood.

Staff
We were disturbed to find a lack of sustained informality in many of the classes visited. It was not unusual to see the master standing up and the boys sitting down. There were even instances of boys putting their hands up before asking questions. There is an undue concentration of masters with high academic qualifications. There is, for instance, a highly qualified teacher of Russian. It is for consideration whether he might not be better employed as an itinerant teacher visiting each one of the neighbourhood schools in turn, perhaps taking advantage of the availability of the 73 bus.

Curriculum

This appeared to be very old-fashioned with relatively little attention being paid to normal growth-points in contemporary studies such as civics, sociology, the study of mortgage rates and the subcultures of Polynesia. A substantial number of boys were studying Greek and Latin. Considering the cultural riches now available in cheap and strong paper-back editions, it seemed surprising to find boys studying the poet Ovid, when for a few pence they could so easily acquire their own edition of the *Kama Sutra*.

Pupils

On the surface many of them appeared to be quite happy and in such an enclosed, competitive society it was pleasing to see how some of them seemed to be growing their hair long. Closely questioned about their sex life, they rather surprisingly affirmed that they saw quite as many girls (whom they were inclined to refer to as birds) as they found necessary. On the question of drugs they were betrayed by their middle-class reticence and we felt it would be desirable if they were encouraged to frequent some of the excellent coffee-bars around the Hammersmith Broadway. Despite the close vicinity of Cadby Hall they appeared to show no interest in the technology of Swiss Rolls. Indeed, one boy said he refused to eat them. Many of them appeared to be addicted to what used to be called 'manly games', and here again an obvious opportunity had been overlooked for arranging matches with the neighbouring Royal Ballet School.

High Master

At times we detected a certain flippancy and lack of high seriousness. He is also a believer in streaming, though not in all other respects completely unreasonable.

We were sad to have to record that the hospitality enjoyed by members of the Commission was not on the usual lavish scale, the Bursar explaining that though there was steamed

pudding for lunch it had not been possible to generate a sufficient head of steam.

It would seem that the quickest and most efficient form of
integration for St Paul's would be demolition and we were
delighted to hear that this is planned for 1969.

There we may perhaps leave Edmass and consider some
aspects of our contemporary culture which many of its ex-
ponents so enthusiastically embrace.

CHAPTER 3
OUR LIBERAL PRACTITIONERS

Advocates of the abolition of selective secondary schools—direct grant, maintained or independent—are sometimes more preoccupied in their eagerness to press ahead with radical solutions and forward to the classless society than with the problem of efficiently reorganizing the nation's schools and the equally pressing problem of what is to be taught in them. We are to have comprehensive schools; some of the more advanced Edmass thinkers are moving ahead to the idea of comprehensive universities; is there also to be something we can look forward to that we might call comprehensive *education*? It is now the fashion to deride T. S. Eliot for his reactionary view that educational institutions do not so much create a culture as reflect it. He was, however, surely right in suggesting that the national culture and mores are bound at any one point in time to bear heavily on the content and methodology of education. There is certainly much talk these days of the need for education always to be relevant to the society we live in—or, as the cliché has it, this day and age—and indeed of the need for education always to be forward-looking. Matthew Arnold's definition of culture as 'the acquainting ourselves with the best that has been known and said in the world, and thus with the history of the human spirit' is much frowned upon as backward-looking and inadequate. When Lord Acton in his Cambridge inaugural lecture of 1895 pointed out that history compels us to fasten on abiding issues and rescues us from the temporary and transient, he was speaking to historians rather than to sociologists. The wisdom of the ages is not much more in vogue these days than is the music of the spheres. Culturally what now matters above all else is change and novelty. Since the technology of everyday living advances at breakneck speed, culture seems either to aim at a breathlessly comparable rate of change or to collapse defeated, falling back in despair on reviving *The Desert Song*. But as we become more technically sophisticated we become more culturally juvenile. The electric guitar is the perfect instrument of both tendencies. The cultural opinion formers—for the most part Britain's *Linksintellectuelle*—dare not turn their backs on popular and progressive culture, which is therefore likely to flourish exceedingly in the foreseeable future. If we look to the past it will only be for purposes of pastiche or propaganda.

In one sense this is inevitable and in one sense, though in one sense only, desirable. The dominant strand in our culture is scientific and here at least we have legitimate room for pride in our civilization. The scientist will nod appreciatively at the giants of the past but move hurriedly on with his own immediate and exacting concerns. The past for him as a scientist, though not necessarily in other respects, is a lumber-room gathering dust. Whether the economist and the sociologist, aspiring as they do to elevate their disciplines to a comparable standard of scientific rigour, should adopt the same attitude is perhaps more debatable. In the humanities, however—and especially in the humanities as a medium of education—an over-nice concern with contemporary relevance can be a great deal less obviously desirable. While it is perhaps not essential now, if it ever was, for every schoolboy to know who killed Montezuma's daughter or who strangled Atahualpa, it will be a great deal more disastrous if we come to concentrate exclusively in our schools on how North Sea gas should be distributed or how a Finance and General Purpose Committee should be run. No doubt we are all a little bit better for knowing how people grow up in Melanesia, but we may also be better for having studied the motives, achievements and failures of Gregory VII or Oliver Cromwell. We may be told—and even take it on trust—that there is a great lyric power in the work of Mr Bob Dylan, but we will be the losers if we study him to the complete exclusion of Catullus or Keats.

There is some evidence that part of the trouble derives from a failure of nerve on the part of the guardians of the traditional humanities themselves. There is much talk of 'a crisis in the humanities' and indeed a book with that title was published by Penguin Books in 1964 under the general editorship of Dr J. H. Plumb. Dr Plumb himself argues in it bravely and quite rightly for the need to recover in history an awareness of human progress. Dr Moses Finley eloquently expounds the revolution in the teaching of classics which he has done so much to pioneer; Graham Hough, exposing the all too familiar malaise which afflicts schools of English Literature, goes so far as to say 'What is disgustingly called "English" in universities should never have grown into a separate and isolated "subject" as it has.' These and others tell us things that we no doubt need to hear. It will always be necessary to re-examine both the content and teaching of the humanities in the light of changing values in an evolving society. By and large this has always been done, generation by generation, as can be illustrated by the most casual comparison of the old Cambridge Modern History with the new. In the present situation, however, defenders of the traditional human-ities are faced with two special dangers which need to be confronted with particularly strong nerves and not too much guilt-laden anxiety. The first is one that has been well called by the American professor, R. S. Crane, the spirit of *reduction*— 'the spirit that denies the essence of the humanities by seeking always to direct our attention away from the multiplicity and diversity of human achievements, in their rich concrete actuality, to some lower or lowest common denominator; the spirit that is ever intent on resolving the complex into the simple, the conscious into the unconscious, the human into the natural; the spirit for which great philosophic systems are nothing but the expression of personal opinions or class prejudices, the forms of art nothing but their materials or their sources in the unconscious mind, the acts of statesmen nothing but the reflections of economic causes, the moral virtues nothing but the *mores* or the functioning of the glands.'[1] In its crudest and most damaging cultural manifestation this tendency expresses itself in a philistine refusal to accept any traditional humanistic values and in the belief that late twentieth-century man, with the brilliant illumination of the *Zeitgeist*, can somehow 'see through' the past. The academics, it is held, can be left to their dreary self-appointed task of docketing and classifying the lumber, leaving everyone else free to get on with building the new society—according to temperament either by demolishing the old as quickly as possible or by sitting in committees convened to plan the post-demolition Utopia.

The spirit of reduction flowered, of course, exceedingly in the eighteenth century. Here there is perhaps an instructive parallel, if it is not extended too far. Michael Holroyd in his life of Lytton Strachey records that Strachey wrote to G. E. Moore in 1903: 'the truth there really can be no doubt is really now upon the march. I date from October 1903 the beginning of the Age of Reason.' He was right in the sense that since about that time we have been experiencing a second manifestation of the eighteenth-century Enlightenment. There are differences, of course—we have nothing equivalent to the patrician element in eighteenth-century culture, which was never entirely outshone even at the height of the Enlightenment by the bourgeois *illuminati*, and so retained a high level of style which is entirely missing with us. We also have a greater passion for measurement. The resemblances, however, are striking. They, like us, were environmentalists—man is potentially perfect and it is only his institutions that are vile. *Ecrasez l'infâme*, says Voltaire; down with the establishment,

---

[1] *The Idea of the Humanities*, R. S. Crane. Introduction p. xiv. Professor Crane wrote before the days of Marshall McLuhan. 'The Medium is the Message' is the finest flower of the spirit of reduction.

say Mr David Frost and *Private Eye*. Helvétius, a founding father of Edmass, would have made a perfect contributor to *Looking Forward to the Seventies* with his twin propositions that 'all men are born equal' and that 'to be happy and powerful is only a matter of perfecting the science of education'. Both periods present an uncomfortable contrast between the liberal piety of their political protestations and the prevalence of particularly brutal and cynical wars of aggression. Both, *mutatis mutandis*, are inclined to overvalue the intrinsic wisdom and virtue of the noble savage. Baron d'Holbach in his *Système de la Nature* reduced everything in the universe to matter and its motions which conforms well enough to our general notions of existence, as does also his proposition that happiness is the true end of man, so that 'if vice renders him happy he should love vice'. If the eighteenth century had a passion for social geometry, this is matched by our enthusiasm for social engineering. As our Enlightenment begins to crack up, we can observe Scientology approximating to the rôle of Cagliostro and Muggeridge mirroring de Maistre.

An Age of Reason holds a low view of the past. Because the past is deemed to be very past it will be sensible to ignore it. Discovery is what matters; there will be no need to bother with recovery. Rapid intellectual digestion of a widely varied diet will be good for the modern organism. Eighteenth- and twentieth-century cultures with their brisk perfectionism demand the *Reader's Digest*. The *dictionnaire philosophique portatif* and the *Encyclopédie* are matched today by machine-turned *vade mecums* delivered by mail order or hawked on our doorsteps by salesmen commissioned to stimulate in us a thirst for universal knowledge by instalments, just as the abbreviated polemical history of Voltaire found its counterpart in H. G. Wells.[1] After half a century of the new Age of Reason it is not, therefore, surprising that education in the

---

[1] Or for that matter today's manual of activity methods in the primary school classroom derives (probably unconsciously) from Rousseau's *Émile*.

humanities is beginning to be eroded by flood-tides of reductionism.

The first casualty of an age that finds, as did its eighteenth-century predecessors, a great deal of its spiritual nourishment in anti-clericalism, has been religion. Essentially, of course, this development derives principally from contemporary agnosticism, though some of our liberal practitioners continue to be understandably irritated and baffled by opinion polls which seem to imply that parents obstinately and improbably wish their children to be instructed in matters of religion and even like to send them to overtly denominational schools. Not at all long ago it was an almost unquestioned assumption that really brilliant children, if their bent was not evidently mathematical, were best educated by the intensive study of Greek and Latin, Matthew Arnold's 'grand, old, fortifying, classical curriculum'. This was not only applicable to the influential and well-to-do, moving from the Dragon School to Winchester and sometimes thence, via Oxford, to Labour Cabinet office. Sir Ernest Barker, son of a miner, who became principal of King's College, London, after being educated at Manchester Grammar School, once defended classical culture in words which, while they would make no sort of appeal to the Socialist Educational League, are perhaps worth pausing on: 'If ever we attain a United States of Europe, community in the classical heritage—a heritage which was originally Greek, and has always remained fundamentally Greek—will be largely its spiritual foundation. That is the profoundest reason, and perhaps the only really cogent reason, for continuing to maintain the tradition of a classical education. It is a perpetual reminder to the nations of Europe of the common fibre of their minds and the common substance of their ideas. Their philosophical terms, their political vocabulary, the language of the sciences and the words of their literary and artistic criticism have all a common Greek origin.' A. N. Whitehead, mathematician and philosopher, was at one time considered to be writing very good sense when he discussed the study of Roman civilization in the nineteen-twenties in these terms: 'The merit of this study in the education of youth is its concreteness, its inspiration to action, and the uniform greatness of persons, in their characters and their staging. Their aims were great, their virtues were great and their vices great. They had the saving merit of sinning with cart-ropes. Moral education is impossible apart from the habitual vision of greatness.' It is now generally accepted that if classics are to avoid total extinction they are in for a good dose of reductionism. One thing that is quite certain is that Greek is unlikely to figure conspicuously, if indeed at all, in the curriculum of the sort of comprehensive schools likely to emerge in the early seventies, nor will a policy of diluting the academic standards of the public schools and the direct grant schools be of much help in the matter. Perhaps we shall have patiently to await a new Renaissance. The last one had a good deal more to do after all with recovery than with discovery. Modern languages are in a more flourishing way. One's aunt's pen has been very properly relegated to the lumber-room; there is a brisk emphasis on the ability to order oneself a cup of coffee à haute voix in Boulogne; language laboratories are all the rage and large parties of schoolchildren tramp cheerfully round the Louvre in laudable, if not invariably successful exercises in cultural transmission. History, if one were to judge by the number of A levels taken in that subject, might also be assumed to be holding its ground. It is not, however, a discipline that lends itself very happily to reductionism, and the fact that it has stepped into the position of pre-eminence in humane studies vacated by the classics seems to have earned for it the hostility of progressive Edmass. It is very properly pointed out that if a student concentrates too much on history he is liable to become seriously innumerate and it is widely felt that no civilized man these days can afford to be in any way innumerate.[1] This difficulty can be overcome by stopping

---

[1] An attitude of course shared by the ancient Greeks who, while having no equivalent of the Socialist Educational League, would not allow people into the Academy without geometry.

students from doing as much history as they want to so that even if totally ungifted in numerical studies they can do a lot more mathematics; and the view is widely canvassed that whenever possible history should be quantified and illustrated by plenty of graphs and ratios. It will in no way worry the reductionists if history thereby more and more approximates to sociology—indeed there will be some who would happily see history become, if not a subordinate department of sociology, at least a minor component of an omnium gatherum social studies curriculum. Then again there is the stern emphasis on what is known as the significant topic in history, which of course tends to produce all too easily a situation in which the Edmass man rather than the historian decides what is significant; or again there is the laudable movement to bring in the history of China and pre-colonial Africa, very well expressed by Mr Ian Lister contributing to *Crisis in the Humanities*—'like Lord Macaulay we may sit in the comfortable serenity of our western apartment, but it is the world the other side of the window with which the humanities must always be concerned'. But on reflection perhaps not 'always' if we thereby fail to understand the basic furniture of our own Western apartment. Nobody can really love or understand history till he is prepared to concede the ultimate force of Mr A. J. P. Taylor's seeming paradox that the present teaches us more about the past than vice versa. It is for this reason that our utilitarian reductionists will soon need to do something much more drastic about history. The dead will no doubt be increasingly urged to bury their dead.

English language and literature are of course peculiarly vulnerable to reductionism and a particularly rich quarry for Edmass. Language, it is widely and rightly emphasized, is designed for communication, but the further question arises —for communicating what? In previous societies, even more crudely stratified than our own, there were broadly speaking three types of language—the genteel, the earthy and the Mandarin or Civil Service. Thus Lady Chatterley or Professor Higgins spoke in one language with a number of polysyllables and subordinate clauses and Mellors or Eliza Dolittle spoke, unstylishly no doubt, but very much to the point and with practically no subordinate clauses. All this made for more or less effective communication with the advantage perhaps on the one side of nuance, on the other of emphasis. Mandarin or Civil Service changes very little. It will be more statistical than it used to be and increasingly allows itself neologisms like 'remit' or 'ongoing', which derive directly from what is done with the files. But elsewhere Mellors and Eliza have acquired increasing linguistic respectability. The delicate traceries of Virginia Woolf's stream of consciousness are one thing, but Mrs Bloom's subconscious is quite another with all sorts of different things to communicate, and Mrs Bloom is now very much in vogue. Leaving aside the Civil Service, which is in a way neuter, the indications are that we will increasingly talk and write with earthiness and emphasis. When it was mercifully decided not to subject President Eisenhower to the new heart surgery our newspaper readers were confronted with the headline: 'Ike: heart swap off'—clear enough communication of course, but notably lacking in sensitivity. The principal preoccupations of Mellors and Mrs Bloom require of course only a relatively low level of verbal sensitivity. It is the proud boast of the *News of the World* that 'all life is here'. If we believe that, as we are bidden to, we will not bother about nuances and will certainly not need to be afraid of Virginia Woolf. Following Mr Roebuck we are all increasingly able to say and write what we like. It will not be easy for teachers, continually urged to have a proper regard for the contemporary and relevant, to ask the further question as to whether what is said and written is worth saying or worth writing.

In English teaching the great thing now is the novel, because the novel deals with society. The world of the poet is too often a private world and his work is particularly liable to be encumbered with nuances. The novel will help to tell us how we ought to live now. We will not learn very much from *Vanity Fair* because the posturings of a defunct and decadent aristocratic society lack relevance and immediacy. We may learn more from *Middlemarch*, but then again it tells of a remote middle-class society and is full of nuances. We are often told in the schools to encourage our pupils as early as possible to get their teeth into contemporary novels, which are directly relevant to their own *experience*. It is not every sixth-former admittedly who seriously studies the columns of *The Times Literary Supplement*, but if encouraged to do so by a forward-looking English master, intent on inculcating the virtues of contemporaneity and relevance, he would have been able to take his pick of three novels reviewed in adjacent columns of one issue as follows:[1]

Tina Chad Christian : BABY LOVE

Luci Thompson arrives in London to live with her foster family: Robert, a successful doctor, his rich wife, Amy and their awkward thirteen-year-old son, Nicky. Everything is new and exciting. It is swinging London and decor by Habitat. Luci is given her own room, telly, hi-fi, dog. It is, in fact, the kind of fairy-tale beginning to any number of those snobbish middle-class teenagers' adventure books. The difference is that Luci's mother drowned herself in the bath back home in Lancashire and Luci was the one who found her; Robert is Luci's mother's first lover who abandoned her to pursue his career in London and Luci herself is a neurotic nymphet, oversexed and scheming, muddled and vindictive.

A cuckoo in this trendy nest, she sets about seducing her new family emotionally and sexually, one by one. She convinces herself that she, like her mother, is in love with Robert and succeeds in arousing disturbing passion and guilt within him. In the end, she is back where she started, having shaken the branches and failed to dislodge the nest. But she understands herself better and has come to see her previously adored mother for the hopeless tart she really was. And she is still only fourteen.

This is ambitious and tricky ground for a young author: Miss Christian was only twenty-one when she wrote it, her

---

[1] *The Times Literary Supplement*, 8 February 1968.

first book. The sexual passages are merely adolescent and sweaty: she would do well to read Colette. Throughout, there is explicitness where there should be implication and cloudy allusion where there should be clarity. In order to reveal character mawkish conversation is resorted to; it is so nakedly explicatory that Luci emerges as both omniscient and inane. References to the trappings of swinging London— Vidal Sassoon and Scott Walker, discothèques and mini-skirts—and an appalling self-love on the part of the heroine make for a cloying and gawky book. But there is facility and some originality; a more mature Miss Christian may get it all under control some day.

Coleman Dowell : THE GRASS DIES

Coleman Dowell's publishers bravely compare him with Faulkner and Carson McCullers. There are times in the early chapters of the book when the reader feels so bludgeoned by gross sexual description, by madness and alcoholism and humanity's decay that he suspects a parody. But soon Mr Dowell's real ability to handle his characters, to draw each of them into the central predicament of the book—they are siblings, gathered to the old family farm for the funeral of their father—takes hold. The pace quickens, the tensions and revelations of the story, though occasionally too pat and literary, are interesting.

Father had been an old goat, letting the farm go to ruin while he went whoring, and seeking to undermine each of his sons and daughters in some way. The two eldest, Robin and Erin, had taken over the rôles of father and mother and managed to protect the others at their own expense. Robin, taunted beyond endurance by his father, has abandoned the farm and submerged himself in drink in New York; Erin has become an old maid, propping up house and parents. We see into the marriages and careers of the younger ones who have adjusted tolerably well to their disabilities.

Thus the total impression of the funeral gathering is one of comedy with tragic asides. Mr Dowell's Roseville is yet another Southern town that seems closer to sixteenth-century England than to the twentieth century, but he is a powerful enough writer to make us swallow the strong brew.

Robert Stone: A HALL OF MIRRORS

Ex-classical musician, ex-disc-jockey Rheinhardt arrives in New Orleans at the end of the Mardi Gras. He is exhausted, dishevelled and suffering from near nervous collapse together with incipient alcoholism, a combination which leaves him badly hallucinated. Following hard on his heels comes Geraldine, also down and very nearly out. Her husband and child are recently dead, her face bears unhealed scars which she received at the hands of a psychotic boy-friend. Thus begins Robert Stone's novel, *A Hall of Mirrors*; a depressing enough start, certainly, but this is very much Mr Stone's aim.

Two characters as well equipped for disaster as Rheinhardt and Geraldine could hardly be kept apart. For as long as Rheinhardt's overdeveloped instinct for self-preservation will allow they live together in an apartment building which also houses one Morgan Rainey. He, tortured neurotic that he is, completes the maniac trio. For good measure, Mr Stone adds a homicidal con man posing as a preacher, three pot smoking drop-outs, a crooked State's Attorney and an assortment of demented racists.

Rheinhardt (we never learn his first name) is the sole survivor of the orgy of mutual destruction that follows. Geraldine commits suicide, as she was bound to do, and the epicene Rainey finds his manhood at the expense of his freedom. The writing is almost invariably over-emphatic, but comes into its own in a nightmarish account of an anti-Negro rally and its anarchic aftermath.

Clearly it is not desirable for all novels to be concerned exclusively with the birds and the bees and there are obviously human emotions and experiences other than those found between the covers of *Cranford*. We may certainly have more to do in the discovery of what, as human beings, we are; but equally there may be something to be said for the recovery of what we once were. Much our best hope would seem to lie in the possibility that the spirit of reduction will eventually work itself out into a *reductio ad absurdum* and that Mrs Bloom will become as extinct as Mrs Grundy.

The second threat confronting academic education derives

rather from sentimentality than from the cynicism which underlies much of reductionism. We may, for convenience, call it the doctrine of parity of esteem. This phrase was originally coined in connection with the tripartite division of maintained secondary schools under the 1944 Act, into grammar, modern and technical schools. Parity of esteem represents an ideal to which any decent man would wish to subscribe in so far as it means that everything possible should be done for all children in all schools. It has led to some of the very best of recent achievements in the educational service, as for instance the careful concern for maladjusted and educationally subnormal children. The word esteem, however, given certain constants in human nature, tends to descend rapidly from the ideal into the market-place. If a boy from a poor home—a latter-day Ernest Barker, shall we say—wins a scholarship to Manchester Grammar School and then another scholarship to Balliol and subsequently secures first-class honours, a certain esteem will attach to this sort of achievement, which will be unfortunately less readily accorded to a boy who, while always doing his best at his local grammar, public or secondary modern school, ends up with four assorted O levels. If you feel strongly that this is wrong you will be inclined to say that the best way to avoid the idolatry of the market-place is to ensure that all children go to schools which are as nearly identical in competence and provision as possible. You will not of course thereby entirely secure parity of esteem between all pupils but by eliminating the really strong academic schools you will be moving forward towards your ideal. So it is that you will always find progressive Edmass referring to Manchester Grammar School or college at Eton as 'educational hot-houses'. The élitist of course will hold that this is exactly what the nation needs in that rare plants need highly specialized treatment, and he will feel it relevant to point out that both France and the U.S.S.R. have a strong penchant for selective education.

We will return to this theme in its broad social and educational implications in the last chapter, but for the moment let us examine the extent to which the parity of esteem doctrine reinforces reductionism in its impact on the academic curriculum.

As can be imagined, the parity of esteem programme, because of its fundamental lack of grounding in the facts of human nature, leads rapidly to much confusion of language. The new University of Salford, for instance, has selected for itself the proud motto *altiora petamus*. One suspects, however, that some of its undergraduates might be tempted to translate the University's motto as something like 'we are here to do higher education'.[1] There is much laudable endeavour in society to spread the benefits of higher education as widely as possible. But if you find yourself talking all the time about heights it will be necessary to avoid confusion between foothills and peaks, between sandcastles and mountains. As the report of the Public Schools Commission tells us, 'Britain, in common with other European countries is making a troubled and puzzling journey—the journey from a system of secondary and higher education designed to educate a small élite, to a system in which these kinds of education are to be made available to vastly greater numbers of boys and girls.' Clemenceau, or indeed any other realist, would have seen the point of this, on the principle of 'extend the intelligent sections . . .'.

What has to be determined is how far to extend the extension or, so to speak, how vast is vastly. We may roundly condemn Kingsley Amis's notoriously tactless observation that 'more means worse' or we may feel that in the prevailing economic climate there is something to be said for a measure of caution about the proliferation of vast numbers of arts graduates with modest intellectual attainments. It is a question of priorities.

To that end it is worth scrutinizing some of the more widely

---

[1] The motto of the University of Sussex is 'be still and know', conceivably drawing more from Descartes in his stove than from the Lord God of Sabaoth.

held assumptions governing the relations between school and university education. Because the possession of two A levels is the minimum qualification for entry to a university the general public are encouraged to believe that children with two A levels are savagely penalized if they fail to secure university entry. As the results come out year by year and 'pools' and 'clearing houses' have completed such healing work as they can manage, journalists conscientiously tot up and publicize the number of qualified candidates for whom no place is available. Now if the possession of two A levels were a guarantee of high suitability for reading for an honours degree we could well be perturbed that any so qualified candidate should be rejected. Any honest sixth-form master knows, however, perfectly well—and would do better to say so gently more often than he does—that it is possible to pass A levels in two subjects at Grade E without any capacity for original thought and with only the most limited powers of rational exposition. To put matters in perspective, any graduate of Oxford or Cambridge is and has always been aware that amongst his fellows are some who, graduating in the third class, were on all possible counts exceptionally agreeable and well-conducted persons but with no great capacity for deep or sustained thinking. Yet Oxford and Cambridge are perpetually being sniped at by the Edmass *francs-tireurs* for creaming off all the best talent in the country. Therefore when one reads—as one frequently does—that X or Y, rejected by almost every institution in England, Scotland or Wales, has finally succeeded in securing first-class honours in such and such an institution one is occasionally tempted to whisper inwardly—'yes, but what sort of first-class honours?' The question is not of course whether it is or is not a pleasant thing to have as many young people as possible enjoying higher education and the experience of sitting on student committees even if their attainments and potentialities are relatively modest, but whether we can afford it. Your Edmass man will reply forcefully that we cannot afford not to afford it, to which those responsible for a number of our primary schools and mental hospitals and prisons and slum clearances, all competing desperately for their share of scarce resources, will be inclined to reply somewhat sceptically, despite all Lord Robbins's benevolence and Professor Moser's optimistic projections.

Another line of argument, already referred to, starts with the proposition that in English life we must as soon as possible rid ourselves of our tiresome national habit of perpetually grading, classifying and stratifying ourselves. There is, it is held, an unhealthy degree of competition. We must altogether rid ourselves of the dangerous Victorian injunction 'let emulation thrive' (except of course among certain sections of the community such as exporters or heart surgeons or Yorkshire cricketers). The proponents of this way of thinking describe any form of academic competition as a rat race. Examinations, they argue, ruin the educational process and are fearful engines, destructive of all proper equality. The campaign against examinations gains support not only from the high-minded and disinterested[1] but from some for whom examinations have very little personal appeal. It is pertinent for example to speculate on the motives which lie behind the following letter, accorded pride of place on 7 June 1968 in *The Times Educational Supplement*:

> Sir—Having completed two-thirds of my final examinations for the Teachers' Certificate at Chorley College of Education I am wondering what has been gained by the Manchester University authorities in setting them.
> That a serious academic course of study, for whatever type of award, should end in three hours of frantic pen pushing against the clock strikes me as so ludicrous that I fail completely to understand how it can be justified. Had I already had a book published, I too, like the Hull University student, would have torn up the exam paper in protest at such a farce. The whole process is little short of degrading.

---

[1] A word now almost invariably, and rather revealingly, confused with the word 'uninterested'.

45

May I, through your columns, ask the authorities at Manchester University three questions?

(a) Why do they wish to test my memory, which I could have told them was not very good anyway?

(b) Why do they wish to test my ability to write relevant answers to serious questions against a time limit of a few minutes?

(c) If their purpose is to examine my understanding of the course of study I have pursued, why did they not give me the exam papers for which I have just sat at the outset of the course and expect me to answer *all* the questions by the end of it?

One hopes that the increasing use of continuous assessment methods will soon oust the traditional examination entirely but before it disappears altogether it would be nice to know how the examining authorities defend it.

C. H. BROWN

While one can sympathise with this *cri de coeur*, which may or may not have been answered by the authorities of Manchester University, it raises certain important matters. The purpose of public examinations is to try and arrive as far as is humanly possible in an imperfect world at reasonably *objective* standards of assessing educational progress and academic attainment. Continuous assessment methods introduce an element of subjectivity which would soon prove distasteful to those whose main concern in life is, very properly, to see that everything is fair and above board and as equal as possible, in that they cannot be carried out by independent and outside bodies. Thus it could be that the authorities at the Chorley College of Education are flinty-hearted monsters with unusually exacting standards of assessment; or it could be that they are unusually indulgent to their pupils, always anxious to help a lame dog over a stile and on particularly friendly personal terms with their pupils with frequent congress in the cafeteria. Either way there could be a serious loss of objectivity when the ability and attainments of the students of Chorley College of Education are compared with others, which might not necessarily be good for parity of esteem. This is not to say that we might not be better off with fewer exams or different exams. At the same time it may be worth observing that if one knows one's work well, there is no need for 'pen pushing' to be described, as it invariably is, as 'frantic'. Furthermore, if one has the misfortune, as many of us have, to suffer from a weak memory there is much to be said for being resolute about a personal defect and exercising one's memory as hard as possible at a malleable stage in one's development. It could help one, for instance, to answer the children's questions when one emerges from the Chorley College of Education. It can even on occasion be a very excellent thing indeed to learn how to write a relevant answer to a serious question in a 'few'—which presumably means thirty—minutes.

Once the parity of esteem programme gets to work properly on the examination system it finds itself confronted with the awkward fact that pragmatic and relatively hard-headed if not hard-hearted people, such as employers of labour, continue to demand some sort of measured and objective system of determining the relative quality of competing aspirants to employment. They have begun to require a certain observable sophistication in evaluating standards of attainment in the Ordinary level of the General Certificate of Education. They are probably glad, as we certainly are in the schools, that the attempt by the first post-war Labour Government in the name of parity of esteem to prevent any pupils below the age of fifteen from taking O level—a not inconsiderable embarrassment to the sort of children able to take certain subjects a year or even two years earlier—was short-lived and unlikely to be revived. Now, however, they are confronted with the problem of evaluating the new Certificate of Secondary Education, the purpose of which is laudably to prevent children unable to manage O level from trying to do so. There are four very liberal methods or 'modes' of examining for the Certificate of Secondary Education, and an interesting overlap occurs in that a pass in Grade 1 of the C.S.E. is deemed equivalent to a bottom pass at O level in G.C.E. Already one hears much talk of the 'liberating' effect of the C.S.E. on the curriculum. That would of course be splendid, but as we all know the great thing about devaluing any sort of currency is to profit from the new opportunities that devaluation offers. Nothing could be better for many schools than a system whereby children can achieve some sort of approximately measurable reward for honest endeavour; nothing could be worse for many schools than a system whereby children are not properly stretched to achieve that which they can achieve by a little extra exertion.[1]

Another interesting example of how parity of esteem and the need for equality is likely to impinge on educational quality in the schools is the controversy which currently rages in Edmass over what is called the problem of the 'third year sixth'. The direct grant schools, the public schools and the stronger maintained grammar schools are able to teach boys for a period beyond two years after O level, a fact which is not at all surprising when one reflects how easily many of their pupils manage to pass a number of O levels without strain early in their sixteenth year. Other schools cannot manage this. The Universities of Oxford and Cambridge—or rather their constituent colleges—altogether naturally like to examine their candidates in their own way *after* they have emerged from the mass operation of A levels. They will argue, and rightly, that a huge national examination like A level, especially in the humanities, will lead to some standardization in marking and will not necessarily be an infallible prognostic in terms of the originality and freshness of mind for which they are looking. The other universities in a very public-spirited way are prepared to select their pupils on the basis of A levels, since otherwise the machine would break down. Now it will not be

[1] The Public Schools Commission is particularly anxious to make the public schools introduce C.S.E. courses. The public schools have not so far welcomed the idea with much enthusiasm.

surprising that the Edmass men with their concern for parity of esteem and their distrust of prestige institutions like Oxford University or Manchester Grammar School will argue that a third year sixth is incompatible with democratic fairness and one cannot in the least gainsay their logic, granted their basic non-élitist presuppositions. It remains, however, a fact—and a fact of a peculiarly irreducible sort—that if there were no work of a post-A level type available in the schools we would lose from them that small but immensely influential corpus of relatively brilliant academics who make a career in English schoolteaching. It would not necessarily follow that such people would wish to seek higher things in the newer universities. It will be interesting indeed to see how long the Oxford and Cambridge colleges will have the nerve to stand out in their present exposed, meritocratic situation.[1]

Parity of esteem plays an understandably basic part in promoting the view that children should not only be seen, but whenever possible heard. The less rigorous forms of sociology, much favoured by light Edmass, will promote interesting questionnaires among sixth-formers in which they will be invited to comment for the benefit of the general public on broad general issues, as for instance whether they agree that in Britain today the young resemble immigrants and the old resemble natives. There is also a strong and developing Edmass theory that all good education is based on discussion. There must, so the theory runs, be an end to the bad old system of 'chalk and talk', in which the teacher, as it is invariably phrased, 'merely drones on'. Indeed, it is widely held that the seminar, a type of teaching in many ways very well suited to small groups of postgraduate students more or less well versed in their subject, should be extended to undergraduates all the way from California to Sussex. Now it is of course true that this was to some extent the manner in which Socrates taught about the eternal verities, but then he was not

---

[1] In this connection the winds of change blowing gustily in King's and Balliol may soon develop into a hurricane.

teaching schoolchildren. Anyone who has had the experience of listening to a classroom discussion by inarticulate and under-endowed ninth-graders in a consciously progressive American high school will not necessarily wish this pattern of education universalized. Its essential weakness is that hardly anybody acquires any information in the course of fifty minutes. It will of course be argued that the great thing is that the young should learn to express themselves. An old-fashioned and discredited view is that they do this better by themselves for themselves outside school hours than by wasting classroom time in a general symposium of inarticulate muttering, punctuated by the shrill and persistent piping of the relatively rare articulate adolescent for whom the most important educational lesson is to learn to think before he or she regurgitates the family view on social justice or the sanctity of dividends. However, these days, we are all encouraged to be exhibitionists and there is little sympathy for the view once expressed by Mr Frank Swinnerton that as between exhibitions and inhibitions he preferred inhibitions.

Parity of esteem, as it throws its protective aura round the educational scene, is inclined to produce the sort of linguistic devaluation of which we perhaps unjustly suspected the undergraduates of Salford University as they set about translating their Latin motto. There is, for instance, the concept of the new sixth form. Quite recently everyone had a more or less clear idea of what was meant by a strong sixth form. This would be the part of a school wherein the boys or girls in appreciable numbers having managed their five or six Ordinary levels would proceed to more specialized work, essentially of a more academic type. The encouraging extent to which boys and girls with relatively little academic bent choose to stay on at school—in itself an immensely valuable development despite recent setbacks—now requires us to be extremely careful as to just how we use the term 'sixth form'. We will be using, in fact, a chronological rather than a meritocratic term. Thus, a member of the general public could easily be confused into thinking that an entity called a Sixth Form

College would be entirely or at any rate predominantly concerned with academic education, whereas this will not at all be the case since it must be increasingly unselective to suit the contemporary fashion in these matters. In something of the same way as the new University of Surrey will differ sharply from the old University of Oxford in that the former will confer degrees in 'home economy' and the latter will not, so the new sixth form will increasingly become markedly different from the old.

Whether under these new and challenging conditions the highly necessary functions which used to be discharged by the old sixth forms will continue equally effectively is very much at the core of the whole argument. What is not contestable is that if you have to provide adequate staffing for a wide number of vocational subjects you will have to have a really large sixth form if you are going to cater adequately for the proper range of academic subjects in varied combinations. Thus, when Mr Brian McArthur of *The Times* describes in eulogistic terms a brilliantly successful comprehensive school in the North of England (which at one point he commends, in terms which will not appeal to every parent, as 'a school that never says no'), he rather undermines his case when he tells us that the sixth form has only 120 pupils.[1]

Ideally, then, we want to provide the greatest possible opportunities for the new sixth-formers while doing nothing to retard the old, and no one will quarrel with the desirability, if human nature can be so persuaded as it ought, that both should enjoy parity of esteem. If, however, there is indeed to be a generous mixing of hugely diversified talents in the same sixth forms there will be three dangers which we must be at pains to minimize. These we may describe as the tree-watering system, the smorgasbord system, and the flight of the intellectual teacher.

What we may call the tree-watering approach to education derives initially from Rousseau's view that 'man is a being

---

[1] *The Times*, 5 August 1968.

naturally good, loving justice and order; that there is not any original perversity in the human heart and that the first movements of nature are always right'. This may be sound environmentalist doctrine, but it impelled Walter Lippmann in his chapter on 'The Adversaries of Liberal Democracy' in *The Public Philosophy* (New English Library, 1965) to comment as follows:

'. . . when Rousseau's disciple, Pestalozzi, the celebrated educator, said that "in the newborn child are hidden those faculties which are to unfold during life", he meant that the hidden faculties which would unfold were all of them good ones. Only good faculties, it transpired, were inherited. The evil faculties, on the contrary, were acquired. So Froebel, who was Pestalozzi's disciple, felt able to say that "the still young being, even though as yet unconsciously like a product of nature, precisely and surely wills that which is best for himself".

'Froebel, of course, had no way of proving that infants are precise and sure about anything. Nor did Rousseau know how to prove that there is no perversity in the human heart, and that the first movements of nature are always right. But if only all this could be taken as true, how miraculously it simplified the problems of the new democracies! If men do not have to acquire painfully by learning, if they are born with the necessary good faculties, if their first intentions are always right, if they unconsciously but precisely and surely will what is best for themselves from infancy on, then there is in the very nature of things a guarantee that popular government must succeed.

'The best government will be the one which governs the least and requires, therefore, the least training and experience in the art of governing. The best education for democracy will be the one which trains, disciplines, and teaches the least. For the necessary faculties are inborn and they are more likely to be perverted by too much culture than to wither for the lack of it. There is, moreover, no body of public knowledge and no public philosophy that the schools are called upon to transmit.

There are, therefore, no inconvenient questions of faith and morals, questions on which there is no prospect of agreement by popular decision. The curriculum can be emptied of all the studies and the disciplines which relate to faith and to morals. And so while education can do something to enable the individual to make a success of his own career, the instinctive rightness and righteousness of the people can be relied upon for everything else.

'This is a convenient and agreeably plausible escape from reality. Pestalozzi described it by saying that . . . "Sound Education stands before me symbolized by a tree planted near fertilizing water. A little seed, which contains the design of the tree, its forms and proportion, is placed in the soil. See how it germinates and expands into trunk, branches, leaves, flowers and fruit! The whole tree is an uninterrupted chain of organic parts, the plan of which existed in its seed and root. Man is similar to the tree. In the newborn child are hidden those faculties which are to unfold during life."[1]

'The metaphor reveals very neatly how the Jacobin theory inhibits education. In no way that is relevant to the problems of politics and education is a man similar, as Pestalozzi says he is, to a tree which is planted near fertilizing water. For the tree will never, no matter how fertilizing the water near which it is planted, grow up and take to writing treatises, as Pestalozzi did, on the education of trees and how to raise the best trees from all the little saplings. The tree will never worry about whether its little saplings are going to be planted near the most fertilizing of the waters. The educator of a tree is, in short, not another tree. The educator of a tree, the man who plants it near the fertilizing water, is a being so radically different from a tree that the tree is incapable of being aware of his existence. If, however, the tree were enough like a man to notice such things, the teacher of the

---

[1] *Encyclopaedia of Religion and Ethics*, Vol. V (T. & T. Clark), p. 166.

trees who cultivates them would be worshipped as the god of trees.

'Pestalozzi's trees are, in fact, a caricature, but a telling one, of the educational vacuum created by the Jacobin theory. The tradition of the trees is transmitted in their seed, and the older trees are unable to teach and the saplings are unable to learn. Each tree exists for itself, drawing what it can from the fertilizing waters if they happen to be there. Now if human education is founded upon this notion, it must fail to transmit the moral system, indeed the psychic structure, of a civilized society. Relying upon the inherent rightness of the natural impulses of man's first nature, the Jacobin theory does away with the second civilized nature, with the ruler of the impulses, who is identified with the grand necessities of the commonwealth. It overthrows the ruler within each man—he who exercises "the royal and politic rule" over his "irascible and concupiscible power".

Clearly the work of Pestalozzi, Froebel and their many followers has done much to make infant and primary education more agreeable and humane. Nevertheless, on the way to the mastery of the differential calculus or of the Eastern Question or of the sublimities of *King Lear*, there will be a great deal of hard work and indeed sometimes much drudgery, often running markedly counter to the first movements of nature. Students capable of scaling such heights will learn to appreciate the value of the self-sacrifice and toil involved and have long done so in the old-fashioned type of sixth form. It may, however, be doubted if the new sixth-former, nurtured on Pestalozzi, will take kindly to the traditionally rigorous system of the old type of sixth form. He will expect his teachers to spare him the sterner rugosities; he will want much time devoted to discussion; he will be impatient of studies which appear to have little obvious vocational relevance or in any way smack of outmoded gentlemanly cultures; and he will be particularly anxious to have every opportunity of exercising his own free choice of just what he wants to do. Now both these attitudes can no doubt co-exist in the same sixth form—there should in theory be no sort of apartheid or segregation. But may not the one influence and attitude permeate, or even conceivably exclude the other? At any rate that seems to be the view of the American James D. Koerner in *Reform in Education* when he writes: 'I would come to the heart of the matter at once and say that, yes, the high-ability student has always been penalized in our comprehensive schools.' In support of this disturbing, if to many of us not entirely novel proposition, he adduces J. B. Conant—'If the fifty-five schools I have visited, all of which have a good reputation, are at all representative of American public high schools, I think one general criticism is in order: the academically talented student, as a rule, is not being sufficiently challenged, does not work hard enough, and his program of academic subjects is not of sufficient range.' Fortunately for the Americans there is of course plenty of time and money to put this right in the undergraduate and postgraduate phases of education, though to acquire the habit of not working hard enough early in life is something which not everyone would treat in as cavalier a fashion as does Mr Brian Jackson. Supporters of parity of esteem are quick to point out that in mixed ability schools good students encourage less good students by their example. As an idea this would have had much appeal for Rousseau and Pestalozzi. The facts of classroom life suggest that it is not impossible that the exact reverse may be true.

The smorgasbord system is a form of shorthand to describe the multiplicity of optional 'subjects' pupils in American high schools elect to study. Mr McArthur in the article already quoted entitled 'Model Working of Pure Comprehensive school' tells us that the headmaster concerned offers the pupils 50,000 different combinations of eight subjects at the age of fourteen of which four—English, mathematics, physical education and religious education—are compulsory. This is very enlightened and a far cry from the straitjacket of an imposed curriculum, based on what the teachers think the child could or should manage. Once again, it is surprising to find that as we are moving energetically towards a world of options, electives and Life Adjustment classes, the Americans are having the sort of second thoughts expressed by Dr Koerner: 'We should put an end as soon as possible to the smorgasbord curriculum. We should, that is, drastically curtail the elective system of our schools (and colleges too, for that matter)... We are the only advanced nation of the world that refuses to recognize the central importance of a stipulated curriculum, and not only just for good students, but for all.'[1]

We may finally conclude an analysis of the consequences of a too rigid adherence to the doctrine of parity of esteem as it affects schools by examining how it might affect teachers. It is a mark of those always anxious to move on as quickly as possible to radical solutions and much less anxious proportionately to listen to the dictates of common sense to conclude that the overwhelming majority of people are like them. Edmass radicals have a tendency to assume that those who choose to devote their lives to teaching set out to do so primarily because they feel they have it in them to be social missionaries—not millionaires but millennarians. There may indeed be some truth in this. The National Union of Teachers, when not concerned as unions properly are with problems of remuneration and demarcation and a unified profession, is inclined to stress the social aspects of schoolteaching. There are, however, among those who choose teaching as a career some who do not, one suspects, regard themselves as social missionaries or millennarians and really do not give a fig for disputes about demarcation or a unified profession and do not in the least want to join the N.U.T. or show any interest at all in what Sir Ronald Gould has to say about Talleyrand. Some of them are thus described in that recently much denigrated but eminently sensible public document, the Crowther Report of 1959:

> It is the staff that makes the Sixth Form. The secret of the
> intellectual excitement that characterizes a good Sixth Form

---

[1] *Reform in Education*, p. 236.

lies in the encounter that takes place there, in the right place and at the right time, between an awakening mind and a mature mind. Staff ratios are important . . . but quality is even more important. The ideal Sixth Form master is a man who combines in equal measure a love of his own field of knowledge with a love for the growing minds of his pupils. Intellectually, he can hold his own with a university teacher except in the latter's speciality. It may not be a lack of opportunity but a difference in ambition that has placed him in another but kindred career. He is happier as a schoolmaster because he is happiest when teaching. We attach great importance to both sides of his contribution—his personal, pastoral interest in his pupils individually, and his footing in the world of scholarship, through which his pupils gain a sense of value and a detestation of the shoddy. Both in Britain and in the countries of Western Europe the need for real intellectual distinction in teachers of the ablest boys in their later school years is recognized—the French *agrégé*, for instance, and the English schoolmaster with a first class degree are cast in the same mould. In Britain, and wherever British influence has been strong, the need for what we call the 'schoolmasterly' qualities has always been accepted. Men and women with these qualities are needed more than ever today to undertake the essentially more difficult task that confronts the schools now that their Sixth Forms include many boys and girls without any family tradition of what Sixth Form work means.

Is it at all likely that the increasing comprehensivization of sixth forms and the general sense prevailing of the iniquity of a third year sixth and the desirability of everything stopping at A level will continue to attract such people into school-teaching? Teaching the top end of a sixth form in a highly selective school is not particularly well rewarded materially but the sort of people it attracts do much to enable school-teaching as a profession to enjoy in this country a status which it assuredly does not enjoy in the United States. A difficult situation arises when we are told,[1] for instance, that if the

---

[1] *The Times*, 18 November 1968, in an article by Walter James.

county of Renfrewshire adopted the all-through comprehensive pattern it would have twenty-four secondary schools, but serving in Renfrewshire are only eight good honours graduates in physics and mathematics. If you were to concentrate two good mathematicians and two good physicists in each of two grammar schools with strong sixth forms you would surely be more likely to keep abreast of the important work of producing good physicists and mathematicians. You might also keep your eight good honours graduates in teaching when they would otherwise feel inclined to take a single ticket to Dounreay. Alternatively you might take a surgical knife to education in Renfrewshire and say that all the sixth-formers and all eight good honours graduates in physics and mathematics should be concentrated in a sixth form college. Social surgery, like any other form of surgery, does not, however, invariably cure the disease and in an operation of this sort you might effectively prevent anybody with really vivid intellectual interests teaching in the decapitated schools of Renfrewshire. We now know, as a result of a piece of educational research, decidedly more useful than some, that under our selective educational arrangements the percentage of manual workers' sons in the university body in the United Kingdom is 25, as against comparable figures of 14 in Sweden, 10 in Denmark, 8 in France, 6 in Western Germany and less than 4 in Switzerland. No doubt we can do better but we are unlikely to do so by driving our intellectually ablest teachers out of the profession by an over-nice insistence on parity of esteem or propagating too sedulously the views on the universal dissemination of intelligence of Sir John Newsom and of Siegfried and Theresa Engelmann. Baroness Gaitskell observed in the House of Lords debate of February 1966 that 'we must come to the conclusion, as the Minister of Education has done, that comprehensive education, even with its transitional difficulties, and even with some of its mistakes, is the only answer. . . . I cannot believe that the Commission which the Minister of Education has set up to review the public schools will not come forward with some good and reasonable plan. . . . I look forward to the times when great names like Eton and Winchester will survive with the label "comprehensive" attached to them.' To which one can only answer that the Director of Education for Renfrewshire and the Warden and Fellows of Winchester College would be likely to echo each other's comment—*O Sancta simplicitas.*

CHAPTER 4
NEWSOM

To sequester out of the world into Atlantic and Utopian
polities which can never be drawn into use, will not mend
our condition.

Milton, *Areopagitica*

The contemporary vendetta against what Mr Fyfe Robertson calls 'the hide-bound grammar school feed-them-facts
authoritarians' which can be seen to derive in part from the
spirit of reduction and parity of esteem and the need to move
forward as rapidly as possible to radical solutions opens up,
as we have seen, a wider cultural debate than the question of
the public schools. It may be opportune now to remind ourselves in the light of the first report of the Public Schools Commission of Mr John Morgan and his friends' hydrophobia.
The problem of the independent public schools has a marked
tendency to generate heat rather than light and acerbity
rather than sweetness. In seeking to preserve some sort of
future for the direct grant and the maintained grammar schools
one can argue a case for the retention of academic standards
against the spirit of reduction and continue arguing in the
teeth of anything that may be said by all the hosts of Edmass
that it is by no means a self-evident proposition that comprehensive schools represent the perfect method of ordering our
secondary education. Even the great apostle of equality in
our time, R. H. Tawney, admitted that people like to 'reap the
reward of rivalry' and was prepared to admit, joining hands
with Clemenceau, that 'a community which is indifferent to
the need of facilitating the upward movement of ability be-

comes torpid and inert'.[1] What he did not admit was that a child's education should in any way depend on the wealth of its parents. As he put it—'the goal to be aimed at is simplicity itself. The idea that differences of educational opportunity among children should depend upon differences of wealth among parents is a barbarity.'[2] He then gives his approval to the idea that the primary school should be 'the common school of the whole population, so excellent and so generally esteemed that all parents desire their children to attend it'.[3] Thereafter the public schools should be allowed to continue, if in possession of a public licence, a condition of which should be that each school is equally accessible '*to all children qualified to profit by it*'.

To the orthodox Edmass man there is of course no distinction between an educational and a social argument, but Tawney is obviously primarily concerned with social effects. We are up, in fact, against the charge levelled at the public schools in the terms of reference of the Public Schools Commission and eloquently argued in the report itself—that of being a divisive element in society. Whether, therefore, you are talking about a particularly strong academic institution like Winchester or a boarding public school of 300 boys in a remote rural area, you are up against the same problem—the inequity of private fee-paying. As we set out to examine this matter we can remind ourselves that we will be considering only marginally the problem of whether very rich boys should be concentrated during their formative years at Eton and Harrow and very much more substantially the tenacity with which, as Matthew Arnold wrote, the British middle classes in general proclaim their right to say and do what they think fit.

R. H. Tawney's statement of the matter will help us very well to analyse the problem in all its complexity. Few men in

---

[1] *Equality* (Allen & Unwin, 1965), p. 112
[2] Ibid., p. 157.
[3] Ibid., p. 158.

their time have more deservedly earned the reputation of being essentially just and liberal. Indeed his altogether genuine zeal and intelligent concern with the fate of his fellow human beings serves as a reminder of the spirit Thomas Arnold infused into Rugby so that it has steadily thrown up social reformers like Tom Hughes, William Temple and Tawney himself. But the generosity of spirit, which he shared with some though by no means all of the English intellectual Left in the period between the two world wars, has not with the passage of time altogether absolved him from the charge of being something of a *terrible simplificateur*. No historian now takes Tawney's *Religion and the Rise of Capitalism* very seriously, though that work, like *Equality*, is full of stimulating insights. But when in *Equality* Tawney dismissed the problem of fee-paying education in the words: 'the goal to be aimed at is simplicity itself' he was seriously underestimating a very complex problem. In the House of Lords' debate of 23 February 1966, Baroness Gaitskell herself observed: 'it is not feasible in a democracy to prohibit all private education; we know that'.

In the same debate, the Earl of Longford, although admittedly a transient member of the present administration, spoke quite categorically for the Government as follows: 'I can only make it quite plain, particularly for those who are not so well informed as noble Lords in this House, that there is no question here of a take-over operation, a sort of nationalizing the public schools by some backdoor or sinister route. If we were thinking of nationalizing the public schools we should not need Sir John Newsom and his Commission and I am sure that is not at all what they are going to recommend. So I think one can rule that out. I do not think any noble Lord here thinks that way,[1] though perhaps some less important people outside this House[2] may be assisted by what I have said. Perhaps it is

---

[1] He was probably ignoring a young Wykehamist hereditary peer called Lord Gifford.

[2] Perhaps a slightly unhappy phrase.

just as well, as these remarks may be read as a whole, to make it quite plain that there is no question of making it illegal to start a new independent school. I am not saying that people will wish to, or will not wish to, but there is no question of making that an illegal act. But, while we all subscribe to this idea of free parental choice, it is obviously extremely difficult to know what the outcome of these deliberations of the Newsom Commission will be.' We know, of course, now exactly what the outcome of their deliberations has been. In our sophisticated society we have learnt to know very well that a spokesman for the Government of the day can speak as categorically as possible without in any way precluding the possibility of what he said being totally repudiated quite shortly afterwards. It was not, therefore, surprising that the Newsom Commission spent a good deal of time, in fact, discussing the desirability precisely of a nationalized take-over of the public schools, as is implied in their relaxed statement of the problem in paragraph 138 of the report: 'There are attractions in this solution, and most of us would not regard it as being in principle wholly wrong, either morally or educationally[1] . . . we doubt whether public opinion as a whole is ready to support the total abolition of independent schools.' Just what is meant by 'public opinion as a whole' is obscure— something analogous, one suspects, to Rousseau's concept of the General Will—but even the Public Schools Commission, however free it felt itself to take a detached attitude to the Earl of Longford's governmental pledge, eventually had to be mildly impressed by the sort of evidence adduced by the *Sunday Times* opinion poll which, as has been seen, pointed out that 67 % of something analogous to 'public opinion as a whole' wanted the schools left as they were. As Saint-Just rightly observed 'nothing is virtuous instantly'. All of which suggests that when Professor Tawney described the goal to be aimed at as simplicity itself he was hurrying on to radical

---

[1] The alternative 'morally or educationally' would not appeal much to Edmass or indeed to Dr Arnold.

solutions in the spirit of *credo quia impossibile*—indeed rather like the executive of the National Union of Teachers.

Then again one has to consider Professor Tawney's commendation of the proposition, which indeed we should all wish to commend, that as soon as possible there should be 'a common school of the whole population, so excellent and so generally esteemed that all parents desire their children to attend'. This, it will be remembered, was in Professor Tawney's view an ideal applicable to *primary* education. If the ideal and the reality matched, our problem would be virtually solved. However, in the English middle classes and also in that far from negligible section of the community which aspires to enter the middle classes, there lingers on a strong tradition derived in part from our Victorian ancestors that one of the great ambitions in life is to do the best one can oneself for one's children and not to make them a charge on the state. As an attitude this is profoundly divisive, to employ the phrase used in the terms of reference of the Public Schools Commission, but is nevertheless an attitude extremely deep-seated in the human race, no doubt eradicable but not at all easily so. If it were immediately clear that all parents were doing the best they could for their children *educationally* by sending them to the adjacent maintained primary school one might happily assume that in our evolving society few parents would be idiotic enough to pay large sums of money for private schooling merely for purposes of social segregation. It is admittedly arguable that some parents would be prepared to go to some lengths on broadly cultural grounds to prevent their children acquiring prematurely the vocabulary and social attributes of Mrs Bloom, but essentially, since the middle classes are nothing if not hard-headed and by and large not in the least interested in what the Newsom Commission considers to be public opinion as a whole, they judge the issue on strictly educational grounds. Often graduates themselves, and likely to be increasingly so, they will wish their children as soon as possible to be taught by graduates—and indeed as they might put it with their particular brand of earthy realism 'real graduates'—without too much emphasis on plasticine and sand-trays. They will not necessarily be Pestalozzians. They will not necessarily share Mr Brian Jackson's difficulty in deciding what the word work really means. They will in varying degrees be prepared to listen to all the arguments in favour of non-streaming but will be plagued, as was the great Victorian atheist, W. K. Clifford, as he listened to the theological debates of his day by the still small voice which whispers 'fiddlesticks'. When on top of all this they are confronted with the probability, if they opt for maintained primary education of adding their child to a class which already consists of thirty-five pupils, it is not entirely surprising that (in order to appease their social conscience) they are inclined to remind themselves of the undeniable fact that they pay substantial rates as well as far from inconsiderable taxes and not infrequently work rather hard for the community as well as themselves. It is not to be denied that some few of them in preferring fee-paying private education to the state provision are getting a dubious bargain but in their very positive manner they consider that that is an issue for them to decide. Professor Harry Rée of the University of York is of the opinion that in twenty years 'public schools will be as irrelevant as private doctors'. There is no more attractive figure amongst Edmass millennarians but in this respect it may be that his wish is father to his thought. When there is talk of selective social benefits and when one is impelled to contrast the urgency of the Plowden Committee's recommendations on slum primary schools with the comparative social irrelevance of the Public Schools Commission, I recall an interview in 1948 with Mr Enoch Powell when I was headmaster of King Edward's School, Birmingham. He was revisiting his old school and as I subjected him to an expression of my enthusiasm for reducing the exceedingly low direct grant fees I noticed a rather glazed look in his eyes. After I had finished, he directed my attention to the number of parents' motor-cars in the school drive.

There is then this strong feeling among the middle classes that they are determined to spend such money as they have in doing what they consider to be best for their children. After paying rates and taxes they will often have to economize—but this is not guaranteed to deter them. There is also the difficulty, as Baroness Gaitskell and the Earl of Longford and even the Public Schools Commission see, of preventing them doing what they consider to be best for their children.

It will have been noted that Professor Tawney was not, as far as the public schools were concerned, an abolitionist like the executive of the National Union of Teachers, but as he put it wished to see them open to 'all children qualified to profit' by them. It is just at this point that a really close and perspicacious student of the first report of the Public Schools Commission—and there no doubt are some—will have noticed a certain inconsistency of theme and confusion of principle. The report reminds us—and very properly—that not all public schools are like Winchester, but it has to go on to admit, though with more than a touch of disapproval, that they do offer their clients an academic education for their children. The public schools covered by this first report, which being boarding schools are the great majority, are now encouraged as soon as possible to make over more than 50% of their places to non-fee-paying children in 'boarding need'. They are not, however, to be allowed to continue their habit of providing exclusively academic courses or impose any sort of entrance examination. Instead they must accept children whose measured intelligence quotient is appreciably lower than they have been used to accepting in their schools. (It should be borne in mind that for a long time now no public school has been prepared to accept even members of the Paget family if they cannot read or write.) Now if under these conditions we examine the composition of a public school which we may hypothetically assume to be happily 'integrated' (to use the Commission's technical term) we are likely to find a somewhat anomalous situation. If you have 40% of fee-payers and 60% of non-fee-payers *and* have to be as comprehensive as possible you will not wish, as the Commission rightly points out, to pick your fee-payers from the very bright boys who will be likely to go on to Oxford and Cambridge and select all your non-academic pupils from the non-fee-payers. You will want to mix them all up in a good social mix, so that you will balance your slow-moving eater of bottled sauce with an I.Q. of 91 with a slow-moving eater of decomposing game with an I.Q. of 90. That will all be good integration. It unfortunately, however, follows that you will have to exclude a number of would-be fee-payers with I.Q.s of 120 upwards. As a headmaster you might feel that this was a pity. A radical Edmass man might well reply that it was not a pity at all in that the bright young would-be fee-payers with I.Q.s of 120–40 would be forced to go to Mr Max Morris's comprehensive school. Yet such is the tenacity of the middle classes and such is their determination to do the best they can for their children and not to make them a charge on Mr Max Morris that they may prefer to send their children at greater expense to a non-integrated public school or indeed anywhere they can find out of reach of too much Pestalozzi or too much uncertainty induced by Mr Brian Jackson's inability to understand what is meant by the word work. We will come back in the last chapter to a closer consideration of what could conceivably in present circumstances be done to meet Professor Tawney's enlightened suggestion that the public schools should be accessible to all who can profit by them. It is, however, stretching his meaning altogether too far to suggest that this is best achieved by first carefully destroying the academic quality of the schools (and thereby in all probability dispersing their best academic teachers) and then blandly suggesting that you are enabling everybody to profit from something which is altogether different from what you proclaimed it to be. The pound in your pocket, so to speak, would not be the same and so far from such a solution providing a grammar school education for all, it would provide a grammar school education for very few.

In considering the future outlined for the public schools in the first report of the Public Schools Commission we may well profit by borrowing a technique much favoured by the great

Cambridge historian, F. W. Maitland, who always taught his students of constitutional history to ask themselves the question—'where does sovereignty lie?' Of course in one particular sense this is what is called a non-question. Since the Queen in Parliament is sovereign she can do exactly what seems fit to her in that capacity with the public schools. All the same we have the Earl of Longford categorically denying that the present administration intends to abolish or take over independent schools. Yet if we look closely at the Public Schools Commission's Report we may find ourselves wondering in places whether the Earl of Longford and the majority of the Commission were really seeing eye to eye. 'There is no question here,' he says, 'of a take-over operation, a sort of nationalizing the public schools by some backdoor or sinister route.' Yet we find in paragraph 478 of the Report under the heading 'Reserve Powers' the words: 'Nevertheless, final decisions about such questions can only be taken by the Secretary of State and we recommend that he should ask Parliament to give him the powers he needs to compel integration after every effort of negotiation and persuasion has been exhausted.' Now to an institution believing, as do most public schools, that there is great merit in being independent these carefully written-in and underlying compulsory powers might appear in the Earl of Longford's phrase 'sinister', but on no account could they be described as 'backdoor'. They say in clear and ringing terms exactly what they mean—integrate or else. . . . In any case if those who value a measure of independence in education want to look for anything in the Commission's report which suggests anything at all 'backdoor' they need only ask themselves the question—who pays the piper and thereby calls the tune? Suppose yourself to be the headmaster of a successful and efficient public boarding school in a rural part of England, a school which we may call Wyvern. Your present curriculum is an academic one. On integration you are required progressively to lay on a wide series of non-academic courses, in order to cope with which you dismiss a growing proportion of your academic staff (that is when they do not dismiss themselves). During the reorganization involved the headmaster may anxiously be watching some of his fee-paying clientèle drifting away to neighbouring Ivory Tower, which under its reactionary headmaster is strongly resisting integration, which he keeps referring to insensitively on Speech Day as 'the kiss of death'. The governors of Wyvern are unable to find the capital to build new workshops, the existing ones subscribed for by old boys in honour of the Marquess of Gameland having largely decomposed. Hopefully the headmaster would turn to paragraph 451 of the Report to learn that 'it is not anticipated that the Boarding Schools Corporation should meet any capital expenditure directly; this should be borne by the schools from capital funds or by means of loans'. To increase the fees would mean a further rapid loss of fee-payers to Ivory Tower. Consultation with fund-raising experts elicits a rather discouraging response. It is true that the Ivory Tower appeal is going well and there has been a remarkable response to the exciting project described in their brochure as 'the new public school where the Mountains of Mourne run down to the sea'. Turning on a news bulletin the headmaster hears that as part of a temporary period of austerity and belt-tightening preparatory to a great surge forward into the twenty-first century there are to be substantial cuts on new capital projects in secondary education. His newly appointed metalwork instructor comes in unannounced at this stage and says that since he is fed up with waiting he has taken a job at Laxborough Sixth Form College. The headmaster, who is fifty-nine, helps himself to a nightcap to dilate his arteries and to ensure a good night's sleep and writes a letter of resignation to the Governors. The Second Master is carrying on till the next phase of integration and the Governors are rumoured to be finding great difficulty in drawing up a short list. Alternatively, we may take a very small, sturdy, but really not especially distinguished public school, which we may call Roebuck's School (or alternatively Saint Sebastian Agonistes). Amongst their fee-payers are a large number of old boys. For some years now—these being the days where above all else it is a fine thing for a boy to proceed to a university—they have been a little worried, as they pay their termly cheques, about academic standards. However, they know the headmaster is trying his best and at least old Grindverb keeps a good standard going in the classical sixth and even if there are only five of them that is more than there are in many comprehensive schools. There is also a good young chemistry master. As 50% C.S.E. integration gets under weigh out goes Grindverb and the classics and the good young chemistry master and the fee-payers. All that is left to the nation is a secondary modern boarding school in an inaccessible rural area with rather unsuitable buildings.

What Roebuck's School (or alternatively Saint Sebastian Agonistes) could really do rather well would be to provide a sound boarding education for 25% of its intake for boys of slightly above average ability for whom boarding education was deemed really essential by the local authorities, an arrangement which would make very good sense to all concerned, including the fee-payers, except that it would be divisive in that you would have created a new grammar school, which is of course the one thing that nobody must ever do again.

Finally, it is necessary to consider the public schools' attitude to boarding. The nature and ethos of boarding education in this country are very much a matter of public comment at the moment owing to the fact that the boarding schools have attracted the attention of Dr Royston Lambert. It is impossible not to admire the industry and assiduity with which Dr Lambert and his team of ardent young researchers bend to their lugubrious labours in the sociological analysis of boarding education. I say lugubrious in that so much of what goes on in boarding schools seems to lie outside their purview. They are much interested in 'differing goals', 'official structures', 'rôle systems' and the hectic emotional yearnings and soliloquies of adolescence, which are revealed with a frankness and fervour frequently reminiscent of Mrs Bloom. One has every sympathy with the young people concerned as they read their Sunday papers, illustrated and unillustrated, and are tempted all too easily to conclude that 'all life is here'. As we all know, the emotional and physical pangs inseparable from growing up are exceedingly painful. But school life also has another and more rewarding side, not conspicuous in Dr Lambert's study, *The Hothouse Society* (Weidenfeld & Nicolson, 1968). This is the world of the classroom, the laboratory, the art school, the music school, the amateur stage. You can come to balance the pangs of unrequited love and even the tortures of unfulfilled desire by acquiring an enthusiasm for organic chemistry or higher mathematics or playing the flute—or, indeed, all three in the same day. However, it is unfair to judge Dr Lambert's achievements at this stage purely in terms of the rather torrid intensity of *The Hothouse Society* or to accuse him of falling a prey to the spirit of reductionism by failing to appreciate that there are many aspects of a school which elude the techniques of sociology. We have to await his *magnum opus*, promised for the latter end of 1969, of which his publishers tell us in advance, 'This important book will deal with sociological themes such as closed institutions, systems of control and rôle structures, but also provides evidence on practical educational issues; the difference between kinds of school and their effects, the pastoral and religious effectiveness of schools, school and home, emotions in a boarding context and so on. It will therefore be a major original contribution to the developing sociology of the school in general and it will also provide the first authoritative account and evaluation of this particular mode of education.' By late 1969 then we shall know a great deal— except, to judge from this preliminary announcement, what the actual teaching is like. Yet it is precisely that which is of such unusual interest to the tenacious middle classes and for which they are prepared to pay through the nose, whatever the National Union of Teachers and Mr Brian Jackson may say. In their realistic way they also know that children's moods go through very rapid vicissitudes and that they will learn, as we all have to, to take some rough with the smooth. They will not immediately be in an agony of parental apprehension if they have a letter from a fifteen-year-old boy at a particularly ancient and beautiful boarding school stating 'this place is a dump', because they will suspect and often rightly that his mood will be liable to oscillate violently in the opposite direction. Yet even the middle classes love their children, indeed even to the point of inducing reciprocity, and if following Dr Lambert's train of thought they agree that Marlborough or Cheltenham are in some respects hothouses for adolescents they may reflect also that in some equally important respects so is the Hammersmith Palais de Danse or even Hampstead Garden Suburb.

Dr Lambert, like Wordsworth, seems to speak with two voices. On the one hand he works admirably and assiduously to proclaim the existence of a very large need in the community for boarding education and on the other he paints such a scarifying picture of conditions in existing boarding schools that only the most tough and tenacious members of the middle classes would dare to entrust their children to one. It should be noted that if anything the state boarding schools seem in his view to be crueller and even more barbaric than the public schools. This is an aspect of his work which the Public Schools Commission for the most part took rather lightly. Admittedly the Commission argued that integration would mean very radical changes in the ethos and practices of the public schools, scarcely stopping to reflect that such changes might entail the rapid departure of most fee-payers, whose parents in their hard-bitten way do not want to pay for their children to attend coffee-bars or engage themselves in bus-spotting (an extension of the existing recreational curriculum suggested by Dr Lambert's team). However, it is more than doubtful whether Dr Lambert really approves of the recommendations of the majority of the Public Schools Commission. Uneasy bedfellows as they would certainly be, I suspect that Dr Lambert and Professor John Vaizey would come pretty close together in assenting to the latter's proposition: 'I do not think that the central question of the public schools is finding enough poor children to fill their beds.'

Those middle-class, fee-paying parents, who resist the trend
of opinion and feel that Mr Brian Jackson is confronting himself with an unreal difficulty when he confesses himself unable
to interpret the meaning of the word work and indeed may
feel themselves less than half-hearted Pestalozzians, will be
particularly interested in paragraphs 278–91 of the Report of
the Public Schools Commission entitled 'The different pat-
terns of integration'. The problem here was that the Commission saw well enough that the overwhelming majority of
public schools were too small to become properly comprehensive and retain sixth forms of the good quality they at
present very often offer. This represented for the Commission
a real conflict of conscience and doctrine. Consequently with
much ingenuity it recommended that a number of particularly
academic schools should become sixth form colleges. There is
here something of a difficulty in that having very carefully and
conscientiously considered this suggestion the public schools
have rejected the idea of becoming sixth form colleges. That
they should have rejected the idea is of course no valid reason
why they should not be compelled to adopt it. To rehearse in
detail the reasons why the public schools do not wish to become sixth form colleges would be tedious but in essence the
objections are firstly the undesirability of stratifying the
teachers into those who are exclusively sixth form teachers
and those who are not; secondly, the undesirability, especially
in a boarding school, of having a community of pupils all of
whom are either in their first year or in their last and all of
whom arrive at an age when adjustment to a new residential
community is particularly difficult; thirdly, there is a great
deal of scepticism about the American junior high school
which would often be a corollary of the sixth form college idea;
and finally, since we are talking about strong academic schools
a good deal of doubt about what might be happening to the
children on the long road up to the sixth form college. It may
be deemed in every way hidebound and conservative for the
public schools to prefer their own existing age range of
thirteen to eighteen, but it is possible for them to suspect,

though this is not specifically stated in the Report, that behind this emphasis on sixth form colleges is a desire to sever the existing connection between public schools and preparatory schools. The great academic public schools are doubtful of the wisdom of severing all links with the preparatory schools for educational considerations, which though highly unfashionable, are rather strongly held. The following extract from the *Daily Telegraph* of 28 August 1968 is particularly interesting in this connection: 'Aggrieved secondary school teachers may complain of lack of uniformity in learning among primary school children who come to them, but for Mr Lionel Burrows, chief inspector for primary and secondary education, H.M. Inspectorate of Schools, there is no return to "prison" conditions. Rather, he suggested, the secondary schools should adapt themselves to the primary. . . . Referring to "serious tension" existing between the primary and secondary schools today, Mr Burrows said: "Too often the secondary school staff still has far too little idea of the philosophy and practice of the good primary school. The burden of complaint from them still tends to be that the knowledge of the children who come to them from primary schools is uneven, unpredictable and insecurely grounded."' This is very revealing in that it implies that for children to be securely grounded it is necessary to subject them to 'prison' conditions. While Mr Burrows's sentiments are of course unimpeachable, he lays himself open to the suspicion that he is actively encouraging the Pestalozzian tail to wag the academic dog. At any rate it is often a great help to a child's happiness at the age of thirteen, if not indeed of eleven, to be securely grounded in certain simple branches of human knowledge. There is little to be gained in turning Winchester into a sixth form college if the boys arriving there at sixteen are still for the most part insecurely grounded. As far as the tenacious middle classes are concerned they tend to show a marked disbelief in the merits of insecure grounding. They are very unlikely to want to pay for it.

It is possible therefore, in one way and another, to suspect that the Public Schools Commission's plan for integration on the basis of a happy and equal marriage between state and fee-paying provision with continual reference to the problem of boarding need creates more formidable difficulties than it solves. Their task was not one to be envied in a period when there are markedly anarchic elements in our culture and when political prejudice, both right and left, tells heavily against the spirit of common sense and the virtues of sweetness and light. Can anything then be done?

CHAPTER 5
WHAT IS TO BE DONE?

A little generous prudence, a little forbearance of one another,
and some grain of charity might win all these diligences to
join . . .

Milton, *Areopagitica*

To derive one's last chapter heading from the title of one of
Lenin's best-known tracts is to suggest that in the matter
under consideration there is much to be said for a strong
element of practicality to offset too much imprecise ideology.

It is not possible to plan a nation's culture—except in the
negative and dreary fashion we associate with totalitarian
régimes operating a huge apparatus of censorship, which after
a time begins to leak like a sieve. It is for this reason that we
have in the end to put up with Mr William Burroughs and his
naked lunches and all those popular writings in which people's
faces are smashed in till they resemble Cantaloupe melons or
their bodies are eaten by ants in the Arizona desert. However,
it is a comforting fact that epochs of licence in cultural history
sometimes give way to epochs of restraint and so we need not
despair overmuch. Even Mr Kenneth Tynan may in due
course in the Hegelian way produce his own antithesis.

There are similarities between our epoch and that of the
eighteen-thirties in France as recorded by Dr Enid Starkie in
her work *Petrus Borel, the Lycanthrope* (Faber & Faber, 1954).
Anyone who has been to the school dance recently will notice
resemblances in her account of dancing in the eighteen-
thirties: 'The rhythm of the music gains in speed and the
gestures of the dancers become more passionate, more urgent

and more insistent. The whole dance . . . becomes *"une course effrénée"* in which the couples stampede down the whole length of the hall. The attitude and expression of the dancers show *"un embrasement si voluptueux"* as the rout grows wilder and wilder that it gives the impression of a witches' Sabbath. The rhythm of the music becomes still more rapid while the women, their faces red from the exertion, their mouths half open, their hair in wild disarray, are dragged panting along . . . until they fall with the crashing of the last chord on the nearest chair.' Dr Starkie describes the emancipated young men of their day, the Bouzingos, as follows: 'they prided themselves on their advanced revolutionary and republican ideals—in Literature and politics—on their hatred of convention, of the bourgeoisie and of everything classical'. One of their leaders brushed his hair up from two side partings into a high peak above his forehead to simulate the flame of genius. Two brothers, one nicknamed 'Le Gothic' and the other 'Le Christ', wore light blue cloaks lined with pale pink silk and fastened by pearl buttons as large as five-shilling pieces. Petrus Borel himself wore a red waistcoat and a wide-brimmed hat with a bunch of motley ribbons flying down to his waist. As he put it in words which would be echoed by Mr Cohn-Bendit: 'I need an enormous amount of liberty.' It all eventually becomes a little too exhausting to sustain, and the fashion changes. When a playwright like Mr Benn Levy says: 'I like to look forward to the day when nothing is considered indecent, because I don't believe anything is,' he speaks no doubt for a considerable section of the community as does another playwright, Mr John Mortimer, who defends pornography by saying: 'It is a public benefaction. A man is never more innocently occupied than when reading hardcore pornography.'[1] But here again the fashion could conceivably change.

---

[1] The *Daily Telegraph*, 7 June 1968. Mr. Mortimer's observation passes well enough if by innocent he means 'not harmful to other people'. If innocent on the other hand is taken to mean 'not harmful to oneself' one would have thought carpentry or gardening might have rival claims.

It is simply not possible in any very important sense to plan the *quality* of a nation's education since there are too many imponderable and elusive human factors involved. Nevertheless, since education is very much concerned with money and with concrete and steel and glass, much planning at national and local level is necessary and if it is unwise or unrealistic planning it will have unhappy long-term consequences. As Burke said: 'rage and phrensy will pull down more in half an hour than prudence, deliberation and foresight can build up in a hundred years'. The educational system in all its ramifications is an extremely delicate, interlocking mechanism to which it is inadvisable to apply in a hurry a wrench or blunt instrument. Opponents of the government's notorious 10/65 circular liken it to just such a blunt instrument and can advance some cogent arguments in support of their view. Local authorities are required under circular 10/65 to plan a complete system of comprehensive education for their areas either by the erection of all-through comprehensive schools or by various devices of amalgamation or tiering ('middle schools', sixth form colleges and so on). Almost as soon as they began this massive task of reorganization—and the officials concerned are not conspicuously under-employed keeping things going in the ordinary way—a period of sharp economic stringency set in, so that everyone had to work away at plans which are either hopelessly ineffective compromises or far too expensive to be realized in the discernible future. Superimposed on an increasingly unhappy situation were local elections which resulted in practically the entire local government of the country falling into the hands of a political party decidedly lukewarm in its enthusiasm for comprehensive reorganization, when as they see it there are much more important things to be done in the education service. An even graver consideration is that these developments have greatly intensified political bitterness in educational matters in many areas from Manchester to Enfield. Fanatical pressure-groups are hard at work on both sides of the debate and we risk involving children and their parents in a power-struggle uglier even than the denominational disputes that so disastrously affected public education in this country in earlier years, and conceivably as bitter as those associated in France with the names of Ferry and Combes.

The cause of universal comprehensive education transcends as we have seen the immediate concerns of the local authorities and involves via the Public Schools Commission the future of the direct grant schools and independent education. What is to be done, we may well ask, to bring to an end the dismal wrangling and confusion which are rapidly becoming the dominant characteristics of the present educational debate? As we have seen, if you eliminate the spirit of common sense and compromise from your affairs you risk eliminating sweetness and light. As Arnold put it, 'he who works for machinery, he who works for hatred, works only for confusion'. There is at the moment too much hatred, too much striving after machinery and reorganization and mounting confusion.

The first thing to be done is for all concerned to realize that there is much right on both sides of the central argument. The advocates of non-selective education have the right too to invoke Professor Tawney in their support when he writes: 'a community which is indifferent to the need of facilitating the upward movement of ability becomes torpid and inert'. Selection of children for different types of schooling at the age of eleven can lead to a great deal of error, although at the age of thirteen the errors are very much minimized. Time was when the rigorous predictability of the eleven-plus examination was one of the glories of Edmass I.Q. experts. In fact of course the debate centred round the middle belt of ability and the inequitable variety of grammar school provision as between different local authorities. To adjust the defects of the existing system would have been, as it has happened, a much less expensive and protracted operation than is 10/65 comprehensive reorganization. But lying behind the campaign for comprehensive education is an emotional drive even stronger than that involved in the need to rectify injustices in the eleven-plus selection procedure. It is felt that the comprehensive school is the most effective possible method of securing a classless society. The common school was essential in the pioneering days if the United States was ever to become one nation (though a comparison of educational provision as between a rich suburb like Evanston and down-town Chicago throws some doubt on the contemporary efficacy of the system for that particular purpose). Similarly it is felt that the comprehensive school is the only way of creating one class—or rather no classes—in Britain. Thus, it was and is much argued that selection for either a grammar school or a secondary modern school divided the nation's children at the age of eleven into 'first-class' citizens and 'second-class' citizens. *Prima facie* there is much good morality in that point of view. It is true of course that there are many boys who would rather work on building sites than be bank clerks, teachers or local government officers, and when it is pointed out to them that they will be in a position to take home £30 to £40 a week or more from the building site they feel no great urge to toil after O and A levels and can legitimately point out that there is a great need for good building operatives. It is widely felt, however, and this is less easy to gainsay, that it is good to bring up together as long as possible future building operatives and future bank clerks and future Professors of Education—and presumably for that matter future deer-stalkers, if any, all in the same school. Also it will be argued that it is a good thing for all sorts of teachers, graduate and non-graduate, to mingle in the same school, in an altogether unstreamed way, so that they can appreciate each other's problems and capabilities. Above all, it is held to be self-evident, as we have seen, by the environmentalists that intelligence is an acquired, not an innate characteristic and that a failure to realize this has resulted in an enormous waste of unrealized talent in the nation's children, an idea that occurred to Gray long ago when he wrote of village Hampdens and mute, inglorious Miltons. As long as any grammar schools exist it is contended that they will cream off the ablest children in any particular neighbourhood from the comprehensive school and so prevent it from realizing its full potentialities; much the same argument will be applied to the public schools with the additional accusation that the existence of independent schools renders the well-to-do uninterested in the state system. Any talk of freedom of parental choice will be countered by the argument that freedom of choice is limited in any case only to those families where the children are fortunate enough to be brought up where there are books and conversation (though this is perhaps not necessarily an argument for the further limitation of such freedom of choice as there is). Then it will be pointed out—and with much justification—that a large organization like a comprehensive school will be able to provide more expensive equipment and machinery and generally better educational facilities for its pupils than a number of small schools. This is a reason why many administrators, often relatively impervious to social ideology, prefer comprehensive schools. There is varying force in each one of these arguments, none of them is wholly negligible and together they constitute a decidedly reasonable case though not one which is so overwhelming, as its more strident advocates continually reiterate, that no further debate is possible.

If, on the other hand, one were to argue the case for selective education, though not necessarily, as Mr Gordon Walker seems to imply, the case for hanging and flogging, one need no more flinch from one's task than does the National Union of Teachers from theirs. One may begin by once again citing Professor Tawney's view that torpidity and inertia threaten the community 'which is indifferent to facilitating the upward movement of ability' from a somewhat different angle to that of the advocates of the universal common school. Just as some children will be denied a proper opportunity to develop their full potentialities by premature and excessively mechanical methods of selection so other children may be disastrously retarded by a system of schooling which brings them on at too slow a pace and denies them the sort of education we have hitherto associated with the good grammar school. We may, if we so choose, ignore what goes on in other countries, but if so we should do so with our eyes open. In current plans for reorganization in France we find that there is no intention of scrapping the lycée, although it is to be transformed into something like a three-year *selective* sixth form college. There is hardly any comprehensive education in West Germany. The trend in the U.S.S.R. is for more selection for the highly gifted. If we are unimpressed by European experience we may at least be prepared to listen to Dr Koerner, who ends his book *Reform in Education*, which has a foreword by Robert Maynard Hutchins, President of the Centre for the Study of Democratic Institutions, with what he calls 'a candid message to the English people' which runs as follows:

> Until you can accumulate some experience, why not be content to build comprehensives (as we did in America) in new towns or in places where for special financial or geographical reasons they offer clear and concrete advantages, or in places where existing institutions of established quality do not have to be sacrificed? Instead you seem perversely bent on dismantling the whole system you have been building these many years. Your comprehensive spokesmen seem to be saying that the wisdom of going completely comprehensive in as short a time as possible is so self-evident and incontestable that no reasonable man could disagree. The certitude of your comprehensive zealots fills me with awe. You should know even better than America that good schools are not created overnight or by government fiat; they are the end result of many years of work by many people. . . . It is both bizarre and tragic to me to see you now attacking and threatening to destroy your best schools in the name of comprehension. Apparently, not even those unique institutions, the direct grant schools, are to be spared by this juggernaut. Academically these schools must be among the best the world offers, and socially they are fully as mixed and democratic as thousands of schools in America or anywhere else. For the English people now, with forethought and deliberation, to set about destroying the flower of their educational system seems to me, if I may put it candidly, sheer masochism.

If to the zealots referred to these observations seem to be devoid of common sense, there is presumably no likelihood of their having paid any attention to the letter to *The Times*[1] signed by twenty-five vice-chancellors—and it is not common for academic persons of this distinction to speak in such numbers with one voice—'We are alarmed, in short, lest some of the plans for secondary reorganization, in spite of their admirable social intentions, may lead to denial of opportunity for the individual pupil of ability, particularly if he comes from a poor or uneducated background, and may have serious results for the universities and hence for the community. . . . This is not something to be feared in the future. It is already happening. It is not only a matter of groups of sixth form teachers being broken up in the interests of reorganization for it is clear also that such groups are breaking themselves up either by earlier retirement or by seeking positions outside the teaching profession. We fear that the result will be a decline of academic standards in a way which, even from the most material view of national economic needs, would be disastrous.' While it is almost impossible in these matters to convert the converted, the case for comprehensive schooling or at the very least the case for the sort of comprehensive schooling that we are likely to get in the foreseeable future has something less than the demonstrable certainty of a Euclidian proof.

It is a characteristic of those who favour tempering the urge for radical solutions with a good measure of common sense to pay attention to priorities and to have a general concern about what is as well as about what ought to be. As Lenin rightly observed in another context, we must build with the bricks capitalism has left us. We are unlikely in Britain in the immediate future to have large sums of extra money to devote to the educational service over and above what it actually costs. Indeed, it is not going to be easy to provide for the legitimate demands of the large number of universities that we have created, all of which like the University of Salford are

---

[1] 3 June 1968.

determined to pursue higher things, which tend to be very expensive. Meanwhile the Crowther Committee's recommendation that we should raise the school-leaving age as soon as possible remains unfulfilled and the Plowden Committee has drawn our attention to the scandalous condition of many of our primary schools. This last is an educational and social problem which could unite all men of good will, however diverse their philosophy may be in other respects, and so generate the sweetness and light which comes from unity and agreement. Indeed, if we could really move forward in a united way in this sector of the battlefield we might eventually realize Tawney's ideal of a common system of primary schooling to which all sections of the community would be glad to entrust their children. As Lord Eccles has rightly pointed out, social divisions are much accentuated by separate systems of primary and preparatory schooling. Unfortunately, there is one reason why this problem is not likely to be easily solved. Everyone more or less agrees that the Pestalozzi–Froebel approach to primary education is the best method of educating little children from homes where there are few books and little mind-forming conversation. Many would hold that it is equally the best method of educating small children who for some reason or other show or would be likely to show a disinclination for conventional lessons. It would indeed have been ideal in Lord Melbourne's day for the children of the Paget family. It is not by any means seen as ideal by the thrusting and energetic parents of the middle classes and by those thrusting and energetic persons who though not demonstrably members of the middle classes aspire to be so. Incredible as it always seems to the generality of Edmass, there are a number of children who prefer solving complicated mathematical problems and translating from strange tongues and generally getting on as fast as they can as soon as they can. Rather than deny them the opportunity in unstreamed classes their parents at the cost of dipping into their pockets and at the cost of flying in the face of Edmass and Pestalozzi will send them to preparatory schools, which will lay an emphasis on secure grounding even if in so doing they lay themselves open to the charge of being 'prisons'. One has here an example of how terribly difficult it is to prevent parents doing what they think best for their children. Dr Leach, the Provost of King's, and the founding fathers of the U.S.S.R. and Plato were all right in perceiving that the family is the great stumbling-block to the radical transformation of society. It is time perhaps for us to have a National Opinion Poll about the attitude of 'public opinion as a whole' to the family.

Not every Conservative or Liberal councillor working long hours on a local education committee will agree that the existence of independent education means that the more or less well-to-do display no interest in the development of state education. Many of them will be disposed to argue, however, that the existence of an independent, fee-paying sector is in general good and not bad. When one reads a letter in *The Times* over the signatures of such notable progressives as Professor Ben Morris, Professor Robin Pedley, Professor J. D. Bernal, Benn W. Levy, Robert Morley, Bertrand Russell, C. M. Grieve ('Hugh McDiarmid')[1] one hardly expects it to be a defence of independent, fee-paying education. Yet just such a letter was published by *The Times* on 11 June 1968 when A. S. Neill's celebrated progressive school Summerhill was threatened with extinction because as the signatories put it 'it now seems that new regulations require that all independent schools must meet the Ministry of Education's standards of efficiency and this means not only efficiency in teaching but also modernity in premises'. They go on to plead: 'In a world of increasing conformity it is surely to be hoped that regulations should continue to be administered with tolerance and even with latitude.' Now these are unexceptionably liberal sentiments but they give rise to some comments which may not be impertinent or irrelevant to our present argument. In the first place, it is perhaps fair to assume that as a general rule an independent, fee-paying school, run by an octogenarian head-master in allegedly sub-standard buildings would receive

---

[1] The first two are Professors of Education.

G

short shrift from Professors Morris and Pedley. At any rate it was precisely to prevent children being exposed to the sort of abuses which can be engendered by independent schools with octogenarian headmasters and sub-standard buildings that the new regulations were introduced. Secondly, while we all rejoice that Summerhill has been reprieved we may doubt, especially when we read in the same letter 'that the influx of children from the U.S.A., attracted by Neill's books, made it solvent', whether Summerhill is a particularly classless school with a proper degree of what is called social mix. Thirdly, we may think it a little unbecoming of Professor Pedley to inveigh against 'a world of increasing conformity' when he wishes to impose on the entire country a system of comprehensive schooling. Lastly, there are many other headmasters who like A. S. Neill wish to be left to get on with their own job in their own way and who are not at all worried at the prospect of any departmental scrutiny of the efficiency of their teaching or the modernity of their premises. The traditional geese have their rights as well as the progressive ganders.

The introduction to the first report of the Public Schools Commission states: 'People hold beliefs about the nature of society. These beliefs colour their judgement of the public schools.' There is the dilemma and as the Commission had every reason to discover during its labours it is not one that is easily resolved. The *Sunday Times* opinion poll, to which we have already referred, did not differentiate among the 67% of the community which apparently wished the public schools to be left alone as between those who wished the schools to flourish and those who wished them to wither away by a policy of salutary neglect. Either way so massive a majority would seem to suggest that there is no great public enthusiasm for a policy of tinkering, 'integration' or quasi-nationalization calculated to divert financial resources from other desirable educational objectives. The independent public schools, unlike the direct grant schools who are more or less satisfied with the arrangements which they at present enjoy, would be disappointed by any such outcome. Believing as they do that they have something of benefit to offer their clients, they would wish to broaden their intake socially so as to meet, as far as is compatible with independence and a proper maintenance of their present standards, Professor Tawney's desideratum that the schools should be open to any child 'qualified to profit' from them. They have been proclaiming this ever since the far-off days of the Fleming Report. That so little has come of the Fleming proposals has in part been due to the lack of public funds available for the payment of fees for the assisted places on offer by the schools. This in its turn reflects the rejection of any overt élitist philosophy in our democratic processes. Put in crude and over-dramatized terms, it can be concluded that if there is a choice between on the one hand sending a boy or girl of outstanding promise from an area where there is little good sixth form provision to a public boarding school where there is a good sixth form, and on the other providing one more box of chalk in each classroom in a local authority's area, the extra box of chalk will win. Except in a very few local education authorities this has been the prevalent mode of thinking and we can very easily see a great many reasons why it should be so. The advent of the comprehensive philosophy would seem to be an additional and decisive reason why no hope whatever can be held out for what are often derisively called Fleming-type proposals.

If, however, we move away in our thinking from the ideal and the abstract and seek a path of reconciliation, common sense and realism we may discern the faint possibility of some progress. The researches of Dr Lambert may be controversial but they are an elaboration of a thesis which is not in dispute, namely that local authorities are exercised in their minds about the shortage of boarding accommodation in the maintained system. The public schools have reiterated their willingness to help with this difficulty in a simple, straightforward manner by offering a substantial proportion of places to assisted pupils in need of boarding if the necessary funds are forthcoming, without any elaborate process of 'integration'. This is deemed totally unacceptable by the majority of the Commission, wedded as it is to the comprehensive dogma and determined that the schools must alter their customs so that there is no danger of the newcomers being 'absorbed'. There the matter at the moment rests.

Suppose, however, *per impossibile*, there developed a feeling in educational circles that this sterile, ideological wrangling is something of a national disgrace. Suppose—and this is perhaps even less likely—that there developed a mood in which people became seriously tired of the voice of Edmass and the whir of the grinding of sociological axes. Suppose, in short, one of those rare moments when men say to themselves and each other, this and this is the situation and let us therefore do what we can with it. While such a mood would certainly not produce any sort of millennial programme it might nevertheless achieve a modest measure of progress. It would necessitate calling a halt to extremisms, as for instance that neither élitism, with all the arguments in its favour, nor egalitarianism, with all the arguments in its favour, should prevail totally the one at the expense of the other.

Given such an outlook, and given above all else a mood of public scepticism about Edmass, it would not be so difficult to see what could be done. We would start with the hard fact of limited financial resources and look hard at priorities. That would lead to an immediate awareness that on humanitarian, educational, egalitarian and élitist grounds alike, the Plowden recommendations for improved primary and nursery school provision would come first. Then everything that can be done to reduce the size of classes should be done. Compared with these two fundamental necessities, nothing else in the schools programme is of even remotely comparable urgency. It may be for some time to come that even this limited programme will stretch our available resources. Circular 10/65 should be modified in the direction of realism. It should be accepted that the claim made on behalf of the comprehensive theory that no grammar schools should be suffered to exist lest the comprehensives operate less than perfectly is unrealistic and indeed wrong as it overrides the wishes of a very large section of the community which does not desire the destruction of good English grammar schools.[1] The two systems must learn to live side by side in a country where there is no immediate prospect of all local authorities being dominated in perpetuity by Socialist councils. As and when practicable the comprehensive school must be given an even better chance to establish itself by the elimination of the small and ineffective grammar schools and the building of properly conceived, large and attractive comprehensives. The proliferation of middle schools, sixth form colleges and so on should be viewed with a great deal of caution. In the immediate future it will often be more sensible and much cheaper to develop flexible and sophisticated selection and transfer techniques, strengthen the weaker secondary moderns and encourage the many very good ones.

Against the background of so improbable a revolution, which in the prevalent mood can only be seen as fantasy, any proposals for solving the specific problem of the public schools move us from the realm of fantasy to that of extravaganza. Assuming, however, for a moment that common sense were suddenly and improbably to break out like the sun in an English summer, we might assume that everybody had had enough of Educational Commissions and that heads of proposals could conceivably be agreed between the government of the day and the representatives of the schools. Let us envisage a meeting at the Department of Education and Science between the Secretary of State and certain representatives of the headmasters and headmistresses of independent schools as later recorded in the Curzon Street minutes:

> The Secretary of State began by welcoming the visitors and explaining that as well as being a very busy man he was a realistic one who always did his best to maintain a strict system of priorities. Consequently, although he had carefully examined the pros and cons of the question he would

---

[1] In this respect Mr. Christopher Chataway and the Inner London Education Authority have set a thoroughly realistic example.

not be able to afford them much time as he had more pressing business. He was of the opinion that it was in no sense feasible or desirable to nationalize or abolish the private sector in education and he felt that such schemes of integration as he had examined were complicated and impractical and altogether unlikely to command the support of the schools themselves or for that matter of the general public. For the moment, he could see no justification for spending public money for any such purpose, but taking a longer view he foresaw that there was likely to be a substantial and as yet unmet need for more boarding provision in the maintained sector. There were a number of different approaches to this problem which he was examining but he welcomed the willingness of the public schools to make their contribution towards its solution. To this end he was setting up a small central office which would work with the local authorities and the schools themselves to correlate supply and demand. He was particularly glad to hear that many of the public schools were willing to take boys and girls of widely varying academic abilities and felt he could confidently leave the detailed negotiations to the authorities and the schools themselves. He regarded it as an important part of his duties to ensure that highly gifted children should be detected early in their school life and given every encouragement. Where a boarding school environment with a particularly strong sixth form element seemed especially suitable for such a boy or girl he hoped local authorities might feel free to negotiate with an appropriate independent school. Similar arrangements might very occasionally be possible in independent day schools though here he felt nothing should be done which could be construed in any way as weakening the direct grant schools and comprehensives with strong sixth form provision. He was particularly glad to hear all the evidence of close and friendly links between the public and private sectors and felt confident that the steadily successful campaign for the improvement of nursery and primary education was at long last beginning to lay the basis of an educational system, which, with the raising of the school-leaving age, would enable the nation to move faster towards a genuine equality of opportunity. Furthermore, having proclaimed his plans and costed them realistically he intended to stick to them. Till they began to come to fruition he would resist the temptation to diversify them with expensive experiments of one sort and another. He disliked the employment of military metaphors but he wanted the education service to go forward resolutely to limited but genuinely obtainable objectives on a clearly-stated plan and not to be, as the phrase is, 'weak all along the line'. Though he was not much interested in machinery he thought they would be interested to know that he was setting up a small central Counter-Edmass office under Professor John Vaizey. The Secretary of State ended by reminding his visitors that for his part he was neither an egalitarian nor an élitist.

Then all concerned 'awoke and behold it was a dream'.

APPENDIX

The following are the principal recommendations in the first Report of the Public Schools Commission, signed by a majority of its members:

I INTEGRATION

1. Independent boarding schools suitable and willing to enter an integral sector should be given every encouragement to do so. There should be a first condition that a school must admit assisted pupils from maintained schools to at least half of its places—by the end of a build-up period of about seven years.

2. Most schools, and especially boys' schools, should admit pupils of a wider range of ability. With very few exceptions they should cater for pupils including those of an ability level corresponding with that required for courses leading to the Certificate of Secondary Education. They should be encouraged where possible also to admit children below this level of ability. Very few children with boarding need should be excluded from the opportunity of a place at an integrated school on grounds of low academic ability. It will be possible to achieve a wide range of ability within a smaller annual age group than in most maintained day schools because classes are normally smaller in boarding schools.

3. Where schools are too small to admit children of widely differing ability over the whole age range, they should adapt as far as possible to the comprehensive system by shortening their courses and adjusting their ages of admission. For example, a group of schools having a common foundation or religious, educational or other bonds might between them

cover the whole secondary age range and a very wide span of ability.

GIRLS' SCHOOLS

8. Most girls' schools are (because of limitations of size and academic provision) less well poised for integration than boys' schools; even if they were all suitable they could provide only about a half as many places as boys' schools. It may therefore be necessary to take up places at schools not immediately suitable for integration until the integrated sector can accommodate all girls in need of boarding education. Schools which are small but are otherwise suitable for integration should be encouraged to make 'tiering' or similar arrangements with other schools.

CO-EDUCATION

9. There should be more co-educational boarding schools, in order to meet the wishes and convenience of both boys and girls, and also to extend opportunities of boarding education for girls. Some of the larger boys' schools in particular should be encouraged to adapt themselves for this rôle.

EXCHANGE OF TEACHERS

13. An interflow of teachers should develop between the maintained and independent sectors in boys' schools to match that already taking place in girls' schools. In particular, a scheme should be established for the exchange of a hundred masters a year.

INSPECTION

14. The inspection of boarding schools should in future take more account of the conditions and customs in the schools so as to judge how suitable they are as boarding communities for pupils of widely differing backgrounds.

GOVERNORS

15. Governing bodies of integrating schools should include

one-third of members representing bodies or interests other than the Foundation.

II DENOMINATIONAL SCHOOLS

16. Schools which are Christian foundations (as most public schools are) should be encouraged to accept pupils from denominations other than their own, as well as pupils of other religions or no religion.

III CHANGES AT INTEGRATING SCHOOLS

18. In order to meet the needs of assisted pupils, particularly those from maintained day schools, integrating schools will have to adapt themselves radically. This must not mean sacrificing important traditions and values, in particular those of hard work, good relations between pupils and staff and the wide variety of extra-curricular activities which many schools provide. But the style of life should be reconsidered. In particular:

(i) There should be more women on the staff of boys' schools and more men on the staffs of girls' schools.

(ii) More opportunities should be provided for pupils to pursue their own personal interests in their leisure time.

(iii) There should be more alternatives to Cadet Force activities and more choice and variety in games.

(iv) Contacts with home, through weekly boarding where practicable, should be encouraged.

(v) There could be greater freedom in forms of dress at some schools, particularly at week-ends. Eccentric or unduly expensive school uniforms should be avoided.

(vi) The prefectorial system may need to be modified so that excessive authority is not wielded by pupils; there should be no beating of boys by boys and no personal fagging.

V BOARDING NEED

21. The only justification for public expenditure on boarding education should be need for boarding, for either social or academic reasons. Social grounds would include circumstances in which a child is seriously deprived of reasonable possibilities of educational development because of the absence of a home in this country or because of adverse home or family conditions. Educational need may arise, whatever the home circumstances, if a child is unable to obtain education suited to his or her needs within daily travelling distance, or if the parents have to move home frequently in the nature of their work. These criteria should be interpreted rigorously.

VII COST OF INTEGRATION

44. The Corporation should have the power to approve the level of fees to be charged at any integrating independent school, and a reserve power to approve the fees at other independent boarding schools in certain circumstances.

IX LEGISLATION AND ADMINISTRATION

48. The Secretary of State should have the power in the last resort to compel a school to enter into a scheme of integration if all efforts at negotiation and persuasion should fail, and if a school's refusal to enter the scheme would prejudice a successful integration policy.